Golden Highlights Library

Firearms

Frederick Wilkinson

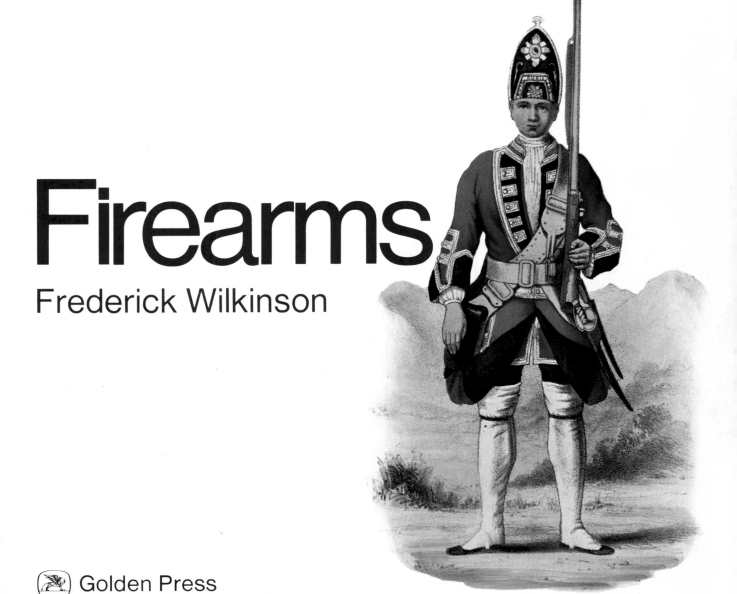

Golden Press

Published in 1973 by **Golden Press, New York,**
a division of Western Publishing Company Inc.
Library of Congress Catalog Card Number: 73–81310

Created, designed and produced for
Western Publishing Company Inc. by
Trewin Copplestone Publishing Ltd, London

Printed in Italy by
Officine Grafiche Arnoldo Mondadori, Verona
Filmset by Photoprint Plates Ltd, Rayleigh, Essex
World rights reserved by
Western Publishing Company Inc.
GOLDEN and GOLDEN PRESS ® are trademarks
of Western Publishing Company Inc.

ISBN: 0 307 43113 4

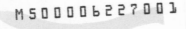
Acknowledgements

All the color illustrations in this book were
photographed by Michael Dyer Associates Limited.
The publishers gratefully acknowledge the following,
for permission to reproduce the pieces illustrated in
this book:
Armee Museum, Ingolstadt: 4t, 5, 8/9c, 17t, 24/25t, b,
28t, c, b, 29, 32, 41l, 45b; Bayerisches National
Museum, Munich: 8/9b, 10b, 13t, b; H. Blackmore
Collection: 42; Camera Press Ltd, London: 76/77t;
Deutsches Jagdmuseum, Munich: 9t, 10c, 12;
QAD(W), Pattern room collection, RSAF, Enfield
Lock: 40, 44, 45t, 48t, 49b, 51t, c, b, 56, 60t, b,
61t, b, 62, 63, 64t, b, 65, 67t, 69l, c, r, 70t, b, 72t, b,
76, 77, 78, 79, 80t, b; John Judkyn Memorial, Bath:
68; Private Collections: 9, 14, 18t, b, 20, 21, 22, 23,
27b, 33, 37, 43b, 46, 48b, 52, 53, 54, 58t, c, b, 71, 74,
75; Royal Scottish Museum, Edinburgh: 10t, 27t, c;
Messrs Sotheby & Co., London: 7, 15, 16, 30, 38, 39t,
b, 50; Winchester Gun Museum, New Haven,
Connecticut: 31l, r.

Contents

Gunpowder

IT was in China that a shattering innovation was developed which was to change the whole way of warfare. In a Chinese book of the 11th century there is a formula for an incendiary mixture which contains, among other ingredients, charcoal, saltpetre and sulphur. These three chemicals are the component parts of gunpowder. By the 13th century the Chinese had come to appreciate the explosive qualities of gunpowder and were using a very crude form of firearm. It was no more than a strengthened bamboo tube which may have discharged a clay bullet, but this was the prototype of the 16-inch naval gun or the modern aircraft's battery of cannon.

When and how the knowledge of gunpowder reached Europe is not clear. It may have been through contact with the Arabs or it may simply have been an independent discovery. It seems fairly certain that its existence was known by the mid-13th century, but when the first European firearm was made is unknown. The only firm evidence is a drawing in a manuscript which can be dated to 1326 and which shows an extremely crude form of cannon.

Black powder, or gunpowder, the propellent used, is a mixture which comprises a basic formula of one part sulphur, one-and-a-half of charcoal and seven-and-a-half of potassium nitrate (niter). At first, the chemicals were simply mixed together, but the resulting powder was liable to separate into its component parts if jolted and it was also likely to absorb moisture, making it rather unreliable. Improved methods of combining the chemicals were soon evolved and by the 15th century a form known as "corned" gunpowder was used, in which the components were bonded together in small grains.

Black powder was used for sport and war for the next four centuries and battlefields were covered with great swirling clouds of smoke which hampered movement and tactics In the 19th century, expanding chemical knowledge led to the discovery of smokeless powders which burnt with absolutely minimal smoke. Since then research has produced more powerful and better explosives, but black powder has by no means been abandoned and many enthusiasts still enjoy the thrill of using it in both modern and antique firearms.

3

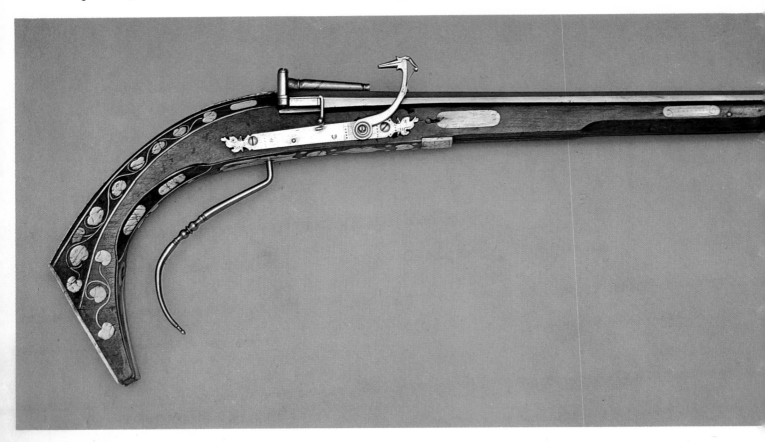

The matchlock

THE earliest handguns and cannon were crude, being simply a metal tube secured to a wooden stock. Powder was poured down the barrel, to be followed by a lead or stone bullet, which was then rammed home. The powder was ignited by means of a hot wire or a piece of glowing ember or moss which was placed in a small hole drilled through the top of the barrel at the breech end. This touch-hole gave direct access to the powder and so set off the charge to eject the bullet. The need to keep the wire hot or the moss glowing placed limits on the freedom of the gunner, unable to move far from a fire. To overcome this, the **match** was developed – a piece of cord soaked in a strong solution of potassium nitrate and then dried, which, when one end was lighted would continue to burn slowly at about an inch or so a minute. This was a big improvement and soon led to the introduction of the means of mechanical ignition. At its simplest the **matchlock** consisted of an S-shaped arm, the **serpentine**, pivoted at the center and fitted at the side of the stock. Into the top arm was fitted the glowing end of the match and pressure on the lower arm made it pivot so that the lighted end swung forward and down towards the touch

This lively detail of a squad of musketeers discharging their matchlocks – from Jacques Callot's series of etchings les misères de la guerre, 1633 – *shows the posture adopted for firing on the rest.*

Right *A much plainer matchlock was used by the musketeers and this one is a little unusual in design, for it exhibits some features normally found on later locks. It is also unusual in being fitted with a long spike bayonet.*

hole. By this period, the early 15th century, the hole, which on earlier weapons had been sited on the top of the barrel, was now at the side and situated just above a small pan. Into the pan was placed a small quantity of fine-grained powder, known as the **priming**, and it was into this that the glowing end of the match was pressed.

An improvement on this basically simple idea was the **snaplock**: the arm holding the match was spring-operated and, at rest, was pressed down into the pan; when the weapon was to be fired the arm was raised clear and it was held in this raised position by means of a spring catch. Pressing on a button released the arm and, pushed by the spring, the arm fell forward to ignite the priming. It is easy to see that the risks of accidental discharge were high and a safer system was more commonly adopted. In the usual matchlock, the arm was at rest in the raised position, clear of the pan. Pressure on a trigger or lever caused the arm to swing down, but immediately pressure was removed the arm swung clear. The greater safety in this system is obvious and for this reason it was generally adopted throughout Europe and much of the Orient, although the matchlock of Japan will often be found to have the snaplock system.

The matchlock musket

By the 15th century, the early handgun, which had consisted of a barrel secured to a simple wooden or metal arm, had become far more sophisticated. The wooden body, the **stock**, had acquired something like its modern shape with a butt moulded to fit against the shoulder, perhaps against the cheek or, less often, against the chest. In place of the metal bands securing

barrel to stock there were lugs, on the lower side, which engaged with slots cut into the stock and were then fastened in place by pins. Many of these weapons, usually called **muskets**, were so heavy that it became necessary for the musketeer to use a support, the **rest**, when aiming and firing. Lighter versions of the musket, which fired a smaller ball, were known as **calivers** and required no rest. By the second half of the 16th century, many matchlock muskets became more elegant and finely decorated, with their stocks, frequently of walnut, inset with plaques of horn or ivory which themselves were engraved with a variety of patterns or pictures. In addition to the decorative features, there were technical improvements such as the fitting of a cover to the pan which meant that the priming was less at the mercy of wind and weather. Sights for aiming were frequently fitted to the better-quality weapons, although the variable quality of the gunpowder and the variations in size and weight of the bullets, must have made them anything but consistent in their performance.

The musket was a weapon of great importance, for its cheapness and comparative simplicity of construction meant that it could be supplied in quantity to troops. Accuracy was not of prime importance, for the general tactic was based on volley fire, and the discharge of several hundred muskets all pointing roughly in the right direction ensured that some casualties must result. The force of the bullet was sufficient to penetrate a great deal of the lighter armor worn in the 16th century. Thus, in the later 16th century, a process of discarding armor began, which increased during the 17th century until by its end few troops were wearing any armor at all.

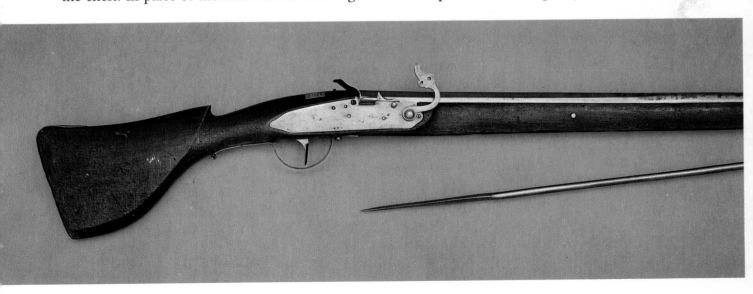

The musketeer with his matchlock musket and rest, a length of spare match at his belt, bandolier and flask of priming powder. From Maniement d'armes, *with engravings by Jacob De Gheyn.*

The musketeer

By the 17th century, most European armies were composed of cavalry, musketeers and pikemen. The musketeer was a man who required some degree of physical robustness and, very important, a methodical mind, for the loading of a musket was not simple and a mistake could be disastrous. Prior to each shot, the burning match had to be removed from the serpentine and held in the left hand. Next, a charge of powder was poured down the barrel followed by a bullet which had to be rammed home using the **scouring stick,** a long thin, wooden rod which was housed in a recess cut into the stock and was withdrawn to push home the bullet, and then replaced. Next, the pan was primed by placing a pinch of fine-grained powder into the pan and closing the pan cover. The match was then trimmed and replaced in the serpentine and the weapon was now ready for firing. After each shot the routine had to be repeated and this was the

A fine-quality powder and bullet bag of leather from Saxony, attached to a leather carrying frog. The wooden powder horn has the usual spring-operated cut-off attached to the muzzle. This was designed to supply one full charge of powder each time it was operated. The flask is decorated with a figure of a spearman similar to those shown by De Gheyn. German, first quarter of the 17th century.

period of danger, since the musketeer was virtually defenseless and encumbered with a heavy, empty weapon. This was when the pikemen came into their own, for the pikes, anything between 14 and 20 feet in length, were lowered to form a spiked hedge to hold off any cavalry which might otherwise be tempted to charge the re-loading musketeers. A spare length of match was essential, since it had to be kept burning all the time, and this was coiled and carried inside the hat or dangling from the belt. Somewhere about him a tinder box was a necessary item, for a dead match rendered him useless. A small bag contained a supply of bullets and a flask carried a quantity of the fine-grained priming powder. His main supply of powder might be carried in a large powder horn or on a bandolier which he slung across his chest. From this dangled a dozen bone or wooden containers, each holding sufficient powder for one charge.

Disadvantages of the matchlock

The matchlock musket was fairly simple to produce in quantity and, therefore, cheap. But it did have its limitations. The musketeer was very much at the mercy of the elements: a sudden shower of rain or an unexpected gust of wind could extinguish the matches of an entire regiment, leaving them helpless and useless until they could re-kindle their matches. It was also virtually impossible to move a company of musketeers unobserved, for the glowing ends of the matches were difficult to obscure and the rattling of the charges on the bandoliers as they marched was another easy signal. To reduce accidents, rigid drill was essential and the instruction books of the period set out sequences of operations to be followed in loading and firing.

What gunmakers wanted was some means which would allow a weapon to be loaded and prepared for firing and then put to one side ready for instant action but requiring no further attention. Such a weapon must also be safe and free from the limitations of the matchlock. What would help solve this problem was a means of ignition that was self-generating. The wheellock satisfied most of these requirements, but this did not mean that the matchlock was immediately abandoned. They were gradually replaced by more sophisticated firearms but the process was a slow one and for the poorer sportsman the matchlock was the only weapon within reach of his pocket.

The wheel-lock

The idea of producing sparks by striking metal and stone together was an old one and had long been used as a means of making fire. Early in the 16th century, probably in Italy, although this is by no means certain, somebody decided to use the same system to ignite the powder in a gun. Pyrites is a common mineral found in quantity over most of Europe and if it is struck briskly with a piece of hard metal, a plentiful rain of sparks is produced. This was the material used in the new system. Leonardo da Vinci, the genius of the Renaissance, experimented with the system, as evidenced by his drawings in the *Codex Atlanticus*. Basically, the wheel-lock mechanism comprised a steel wheel some quarter of an inch or so in thickness and with the edge grooved and cross-cut. This was connected, by means of a small link chain, to a large V-spring. By means of a lug projecting from the axis of the wheel, and a square-cut key which could be fitted over the lug, the wheel was rotated, thus compressing, by way of the small chain, the heavy V-spring. As the wheel was turned, a small metal arm, the **sear**, activated by a spring, slipped into a recess at the side of the wheel, locking it. The wheel was so positioned that its rim formed part of the base of the priming pan. An arm holding a piece of pyrites was now swung forward so that the mineral was pressed into the pan and priming powder, against the edge of the wheel. When the trigger was pressed, the sear was withdrawn from the recess on the wheel, the V-spring, by way of the small metal link, exerted pressure on the wheel and caused it to rotate rapidly. The roughened edge which bore against the pyrites produced sparks which ignited the priming and so fired the main charge.

The system fulfilled most of the requirements of the shooter. The weapon could be loaded and the wheel spanned, that is to say, turned to place the spring under tension; it could be primed and left to one side for as long as was necessary and yet, when picked up, was ready for instant use. The wheel-lock had one other great advantage in that the arm (known as the **dog-head**) holding the pyrites could be swung clear of the pan and thus make the firearm completely safe. If the trigger were pressed and the wheel rotated no sparks were produced, since it was not engaged with the pyrites and the weapon would not fire. Pan covers were fitted to guard the priming.

A Tschinke, named after the town Teschen (Cieszyn) dating from about 1630. It has the typical large, shaped trigger guard as well as the characteristic external mainspring.

Right *Detail of wheel-lock from a fine pistol of the early 17th century. The wheelcover is of gilt as is the pan release stud and the holding plate for cock and spring.*

Below *Good-quality wheel-lock pistol of the late 16th century. The dog-head is in the fully withdrawn position, rendering the weapon safe from the possibility of accidental discharge. The lock plate is long and the safety catch, later discarded as superfluous, may be seen at the end nearest the butt. Inlay is used to decorate the walnut stock.*

Bottom *French wheel-lock signed "Jean Henequin à Metz" and dated 1621. The lockplate is smaller than those found on later weapons and the stock has the characteristic shape of this period.*

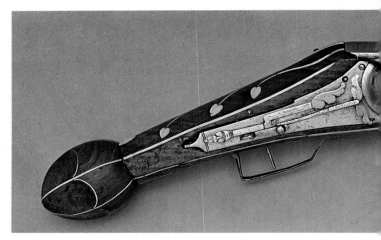

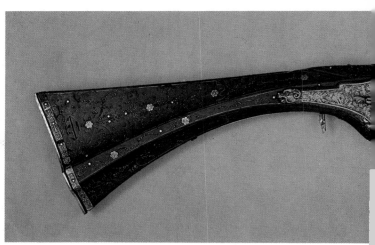

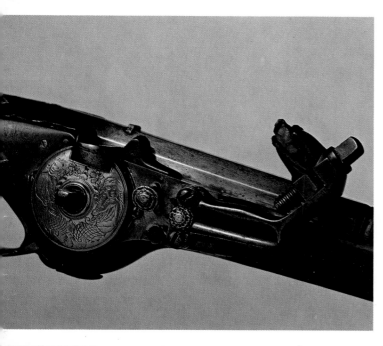

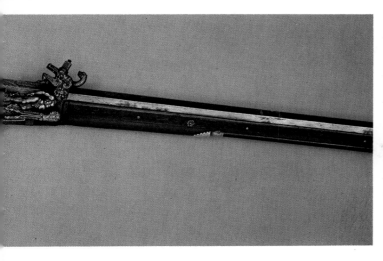

The wheel-lock pistol

Two advantages of the wheel-lock mechanism were that it could be produced in any size and that it dispensed with the trailing, glowing match. Gunsmiths were now able to produce weapons small enough to be carried about the person and so the **pistol** was evolved. The name possibly derives from the Italian town of Pistoia, where the weapons became popular. A form of the town's name may have become attached to the article.

Wheel-lock pistols were, by the mid-16th century, frequently carried by horsemen but since most were single-shot weapons it became common practice to carry a pair, usually in holsters at the front of the saddle. Many authorities issued strict ordinances about the carrying of pistols. The limitation of being able to fire only a single shot was one that exercised the inventiveness of the gunsmith and many ingenious, often impracticable, ideas were advanced to overcome it. Probably the most reliable was to fit two pistols on to one stock. Two barrels were fitted, usually one above the other, each with its own lock. On others, twin wheels were mounted on a single plate so that each activated one barrel. Sometimes a single trigger was, by different pressures, made to operate the locks; on others there were separate triggers for each lock. Another and more hazardous system was that known as **superimposed charges**: in a single barrel, a charge of powder was loaded together with a ball; on top of this went a circular wad which closed the barrel; on top of this went another charge of powder and another ball; each was now, in theory, isolated one from the other. Separate touch holes to coincide with each charge were fitted and then, by any one of a variety of systems, the charge nearest the muzzle was fired first and the wad effectively prevented any flash or flame penetrating to the second shot, which could then be fired at will. It is a matter for conjecture as to how often the wad proved ineffective and both charges detonated together.

In addition to multi-shot weapons, combined weapons became popular, and small wheel-lock pistols were fitted on to maces, swords and even cross-bows.

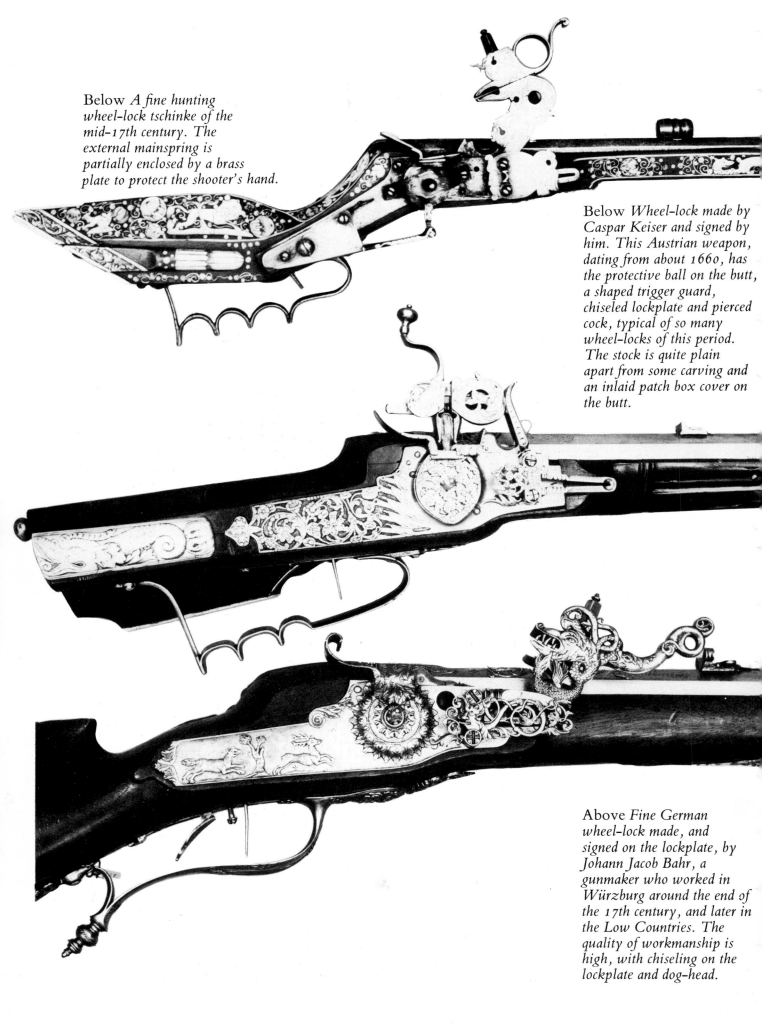

Below *A fine hunting wheel-lock tschinke of the mid-17th century. The external mainspring is partially enclosed by a brass plate to protect the shooter's hand.*

Below *Wheel-lock made by Caspar Keiser and signed by him. This Austrian weapon, dating from about 1660, has the protective ball on the butt, a shaped trigger guard, chiseled lockplate and pierced cock, typical of so many wheel-locks of this period. The stock is quite plain apart from some carving and an inlaid patch box cover on the butt.*

Above *Fine German wheel-lock made, and signed on the lockplate, by Johann Jacob Bahr, a gunmaker who worked in Würzburg around the end of the 17th century, and later in the Low Countries. The quality of workmanship is high, with chiseling on the lockplate and dog-head.*

Development of the wheel-lock

Early wheel-lock mechanisms were fairly crude and there were modifications over the centuries. At first, the mainspring and chain were fitted outside the lockplate, but the obvious risk of damage soon persuaded the gunsmiths that there were great advantages in fitting them on the inside. The stock, cut to accommodate these fittings, gave protection against damage and this became common practice. For some obscure reason this was not the case with a class of firearms produced in the area of Teschen (Cieszyn), on what is now the Polish-Czech border, for they used the older system. Known as **tschinkes**, these hunting rifles are characterized by a graceful, light appearance and by the mainspring being fitted on the outside of the lock. The butt has a pronounced curve and was designed to be held not against the shoulder but against the cheek. There are internal differences in the mechanism as well, for the sear which engages with the wheel has to be pushed home manually and does not engage automatically as on most wheel-locks. The advantage of the system was that when the trigger was pressed, the sear was pulled clear of the wheel and did not press on the wheel while it was rotating – this ensured a slightly quicker rotation and, therefore, a more plentiful supply of sparks and a surer fire. Tschinkes were light and fired a comparatively small bullet, anything from $\frac{1}{4}$ to $\frac{2}{5}$ of an inch in diameter. Early wheel-locks had a pan cover which had to be operated manually, but this meant that there was always a danger of forgetting to do so, and automatic opening was very soon incorporated. Another feature of early wheel-locks was the attachment of safety catches on the lock plate, later abandoned.

Further refinements in design were introduced, including a raised projection at the rear of the pan intended to reduce the chances of odd sparks blowing on to the shooter's face. A few wheel-locks were made with internal devices that dispensed with the need for a separate spanner to wind the wheel. Most utilized the dog-head as a lever so that if it was pulled back and then returned, the mainspring was placed under tension. The complexity of these devices rendered them expensive and, therefore, limited in demand and the vast majority of wheel-locks had to be wound, or spanned, by means of a key which fitted over the central lug of the wheel.

Germany was the prime supplier of wheel-locks, although Italian and French gunsmiths did produce them. Those of France adopted a different method of fitting in the mainspring: it was free of the lockplate and attached to the inside of the stock.

Wheel-lock decoration

Two of the prime qualities of the matchlock were simplicity and cheapness of construction, neither of which could be said to apply to the wheel-lock. The internal mechanism called for some considerable degree of competence on the part of the gunmaker and made the weapon expensive.

For the moneyed sportsman there was often a desire to impress, and with this in mind, gunmakers were asked to decorate the weapon. The lockplate, with its large, flat surface, invited engraving and hunting, classical and martial scenes were favorite themes. Similarly the cock, or dog-head, offered an opportunity for the metal worker to chisel it into a variety of figures including animals, gods and soldiers. The stock was frequently of walnut and was embellished with inlay of various types. Plaques of ivory, horn or mother-of-pearl were set into the stock. Often, these were themselves embellished with skilfully incised patterns and cameos or with an inlay of metal wire.

The stock was obviously rather delicate and rough handling would damage it, so most of the guns had a small metal ball fitted at the tip of the butt in order that it could be stood on end without damage to the wood. On many of the wheel-locks the wheel was enclosed within a perforated cover, often of gilt. To reduce the chance of accidental discharge, a guard of curved metal wire, or a bar was fitted around the trigger and on the pistols.

One of the reasons for inaccuracies was "snatching" at the trigger at the moment of firing and the effect was greatest when a strong pull was necessary to operate the trigger. In order to correct such inaccuracies, better quality sporting guns were fitted with a **set,** or **hair trigger,** a small mechanism which could be set so that an absolute minimum of pressure was needed to activate the trigger, so reducing the chances of going off aim. Many of these wheel-locks had a separate lid which slid into grooves in the butt and covered a recess cut into the stock. These contained compartments, which were usually known as patch boxes.

Barrels were usually octagonal in section and, apart from sights, were most often left plain, but some were decorated with chiseling.

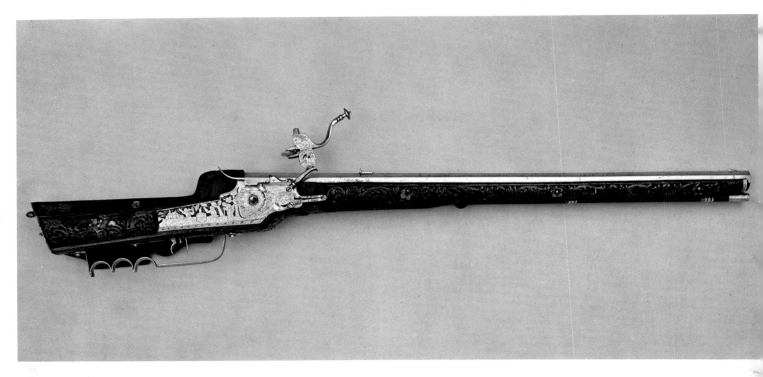

The snaphaunce

WITH the adoption of the wheel-lock mechanism, weapons were becoming more lethal and, at the same time, more beautiful. The pistol became a popular weapon with cavalry, bodyguards and less savory characters, such as assassins. For the sportsman and soldier the wheel-lock gave freedom of movement, since he was no longer hampered by awkward and dangerous lengths of glowing match. However, the system was by no means perfect and prompted the gunmakers to search for simpler means of ignition. The wheel-lock's intricate mechanism meant that it was subject to mechanical failure (contemporary accounts refer to it jamming on occasions). If a breakage occurred, then it was beyond the capabilities of a soldier—even a camp armorer—to effect a quick repair.

The principle of friction ignition was obviously a sound one but what was needed was a simpler method of obtaining it. Around the middle of the 16th century, there appeared the first locks employing a new, simpler and much cheaper method. The earliest known examples occurred in Scandinavia about 1545-50. A "V" mainspring, fitted on the outside of the lock, exerted pressure on the bottom tip (the toe) of an arm (the cock) which, at the opposite end, held a piece of flint between two jaws. Situated above the pan was a small, vertical, steel plate fitted at the end of a pivoted arm which was under tension from a spring. If the cock were pulled back and then released by pressing on the trigger, it swung forward and down through an arc which allowed the piece of

flint to scrape down the face of the piece of steel. Friction produced sparks which fell into and ignited the priming; at the same time, the cock falling forward pushed the arm and plate away from the pan. This mechanism had the great virtue of simplicity: it could be manufactured or repaired by any competent smith.

Although rather crude in appearance, this new Scandinavian or Baltic lock was practical and efficient—its long working life alone was proof of that. Internally, the mechanism was simple and the flint easily replaceable. This combination of separate pan cover and steel is known by collectors as the **snaphaunce**, a name which is usually taken to be derived from the Dutch *snap hann* meaning "pecking cock", because of the dipping motion of the cock as it swung forward against the steel.

The Dutch snaphaunce had a large lockplate, with the pan in the form of a half cylinder with a circular plate at the end. The cock was S-shaped and the flint was gripped between two jaws, adjustable by means of a screw. To prevent the lower edge of the cock swinging forward and banging against the edge of the pan, a small metal block, the buffer, was fitted to the lockplate. In front of the pan was the steel fitted at the end of an arm, the tip of which pressed against a small V-shaped spring which held it in position above the pan or pushed it forward and clear of the pan. A pan cover was usual, although some were manually operated and others automatically activated.

Operation of the lock was simple with a shaped metal block, the tumbler, attached on the inside of the lockplate to the shank of the cock and bearing down on a main spring.

Opposite *A 17th-century wheel-lock rifle with stock, carved and embellished with paint, whilst the chiseled lock shows a rural scene of merrymaking. The lock has a set trigger.*

Below *Ivory plaques are set into the carved stock of this 17th-century wheel-lock which also has a carved ivory cover to the patch box in the butt.*

The lock has been blued and engraved and bears the initials "MZ".

Bottom *Although out of date by the early 17th century, some wheel-lock weapons were made long after this period and this fine example is of 18th century manufacture. There is carving on the stock as well as some very fine-quality chiseled steel inlay.*

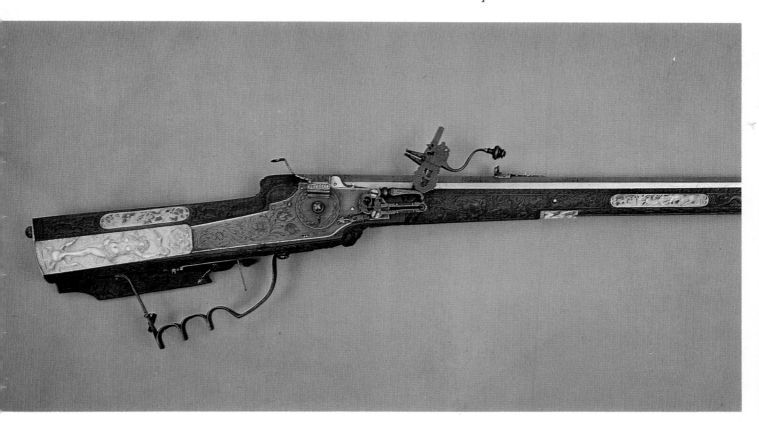

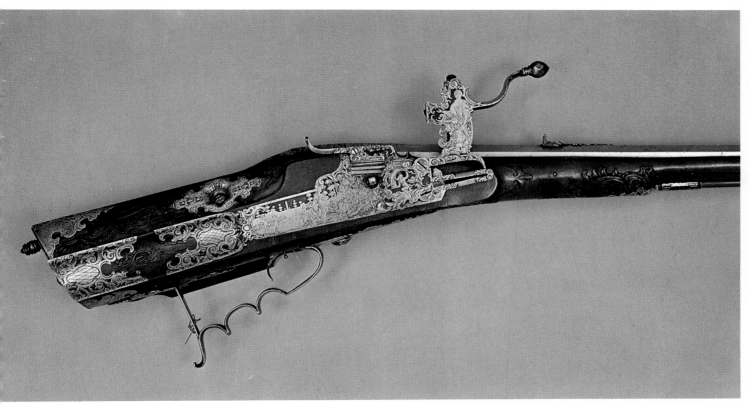

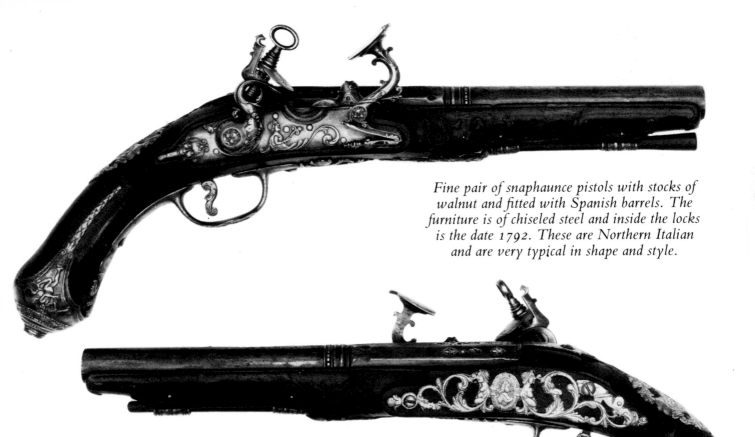

Fine pair of snaphaunce pistols with stocks of walnut and fitted with Spanish barrels. The furniture is of chiseled steel and inside the locks is the date 1792. These are Northern Italian and are very typical in shape and style.

Pulling back the cock caused the tumbler to rotate and compress the spring and, at the same time, a metal arm, the sear, projected, by way of a small hole, through the lockplate to engage with the tip of the cock and hold it in the upright position. The trigger engaged with the sear and as this was withdrawn by pressure on the trigger, the spring forced the cock forward, the flint scraped along the steel and generated sparks to fire the priming.

Variations on the Dutch snaphaunce were used on Scottish firearms of the 17th century and on Arab muskets made during the following three centuries.

Throughout most of Europe, the snaphaunce was displaced by simpler, more efficient systems during the 17th century, but in Italy it remained popular. The area around Brescia, between Milan and Verona in Northern Italy, had acquired a reputation for the fine quality of the metal work produced by the local craftsmen. Much of this skill was given over to the production of well-made and beautifully decorated snaphaunces. The entire lock had a more sophisticated appearance than that of the Dutch snaphaunce and the internal mechanism was slightly more complex. The lockplates were smaller than the Dutch variety and the cock was more graceful–frequently chiseled with high relief motifs, as was the arm of the steel.

Internally, the mechanism was very similar to that of the flintlock and almost invariably had an internal link automatically opening the pan cover. Barrels, triggers and the metal fittings of the Brescian firearms were usually enriched with chiseling while the stocks often had steel wire inlay decoration. Most of the surviving examples of these fine-quality Italian firearms date from the late 17th and early 18th centuries. It is not clear why this obsolete lock should have remained so popular at such a late period in firearm development.

When the Scandinavian and Dutch snaphaunces made their appearance, their superiority over the wheel-lock was soon apparent to the gunmakers, but improvements on the basic design were soon being made. One of the weak points in the design of the snaphaunce was the pan cover; if manually operated it was easily forgotten in a moment of stress, perhaps with fatal results. If automatically operated, there was the ever-present danger of mechanical failure, again with the same accompanying risk. If only some simple but essentially foolproof way of opening the pan for every shot could be devised, the lock would be immensely improved. The system which eventually gained acceptance was that known as the flintlock.

The flintlock

THE secret of the flintlock was the combining of steel and pan cover into a single, L-shaped piece of metal, known at various times, as the steel or hammer, but by most modern collectors as the frizzen. The lower, shorter arm of the frizzen was the pan cover and the longer, upright arm served as the steel. A small frizzen spring held it either in the closed position, ready for firing, or in an open, safe position well clear of the pan.

Internally, the mechanism differed from the earlier snaphaunce for the metal arm, the sear, did not pass through the lockplate but acted directly on the tumbler attached, by way of a shank, to the cock. The action was simple, for the tumbler had two slots cut into its rim against which the tip of the sear pressed. As the tumbler rotated, the sear engaged with the first slot which was so sited and cut that pressure on the trigger could not disengage it. This position was known as half cock and was intended as a safety device, since the firearm could not be fired while this position was held. If the cock were now to be pulled further back, so rotating the tumbler, the sear was automatically disengaged and slipped into the second notch, the full cock position. If the trigger were now pressed, it disengaged the sear from this slot and, pressed by a mainspring also acting directly on the tumbler, the cock was made to swing forward and so to strike sparks from the frizzen. The pressure on the steel by the flint and cock caused it to tip up on the pivot at the tip of the short arm, so exposing the priming and allowing the sparks to fall into it. The action was simple, virtually foolproof and also safe. The number of moving parts was very small and the making of each of them was within the capability of any competent metal worker. There were variations in detail and design, but the basic flintlock system was to remain in common use until the middle of the 19th century.

The flintlock could be made to fit on the left or right of a stock in any size and was indeed fitted to every conceivable type of firearm, ranging from tiny pistols that would slip into an inside pocket to enormous cannon carried by ships or fitted in forts.

If there is any one man with a claim to being the inventor of the flintlock, it is Marin Le Bourgeoys, born about the middle of the 16th century in Normandy and appointed to the court of Henri IV in 1598. He was soon concerned with the gun trade, for by 1606 he is

Top *A snaphaunce lock from North Italy made about the middle of 17th century. It is engraved with simple foliage pattern and birds. The separate arm and pan cover can clearly be seen especially when the lock is compared with the two lower Miguelet locks of the end of the 17th century.*

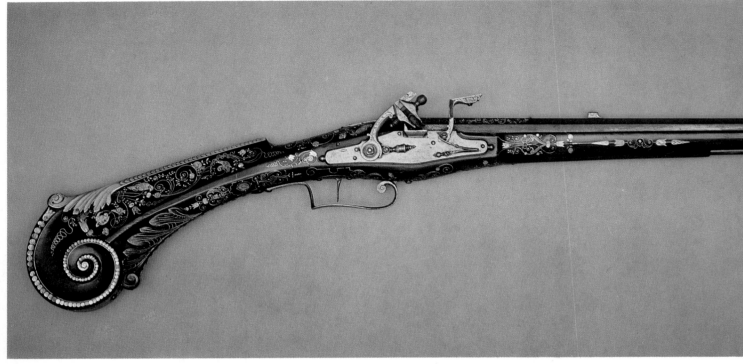

recorded as supplying some weapons to the king, including a firearm, a cross bow and even the design of an airgun. In 1608 he took up residence in the Louvre in Paris, where he was described as being concerned with "mechanical inventions". A fine gun in the Hermitage Museum, Leningrad, bearing Le Bourgeoys' name and fitted with a flintlock, can be dated to about 1610, and is the earliest known example of this type of lock.

Whether Le Bourgeoys developed the lock quite independently, or had knowledge of earlier mechanisms of a similar design, is not known. Locks with combined steel and pan covers were made before the 17th century and snaphaunces using a tumbler and internally operating sear were produced during the 16th century. To Le Bourgeoys may certainly go the honor of being the first known gunmaker to combine the two features.

Early flintlocks are recognizable by their flat lockplate and cock, both with a rectangular section and resembling the snaphaunce in having the buffer fitted (although this feature was generally dropped after about 1630). Early cocks were secured to the internal tumbler by means of a nut and bolt which passed through the cock and tumbler, but around the middle of the 17th century a simpler system was adopted. The tumbler was made with a square-cut shank projecting on one side; this passed through the lockplate to engage with a square-cut hole in the cock, a screw then being inserted and tightened to make a good, simple joint. Another improvement which appeared around the mid-17th century was the bridle—simply a shaped piece of metal fitted on the inside of the lockplate and supporting one end of the tumbler.

The flintlock's use until about 1630 seems to have been limited to Paris and it is only from about 1640 that it seems to have appeared outside France at all. In England, it was uncommon during the English Civil Wars, when the infantry were still armed with matchlock muskets and the cavalry were using the wheel lock. Some of the leaders, however, are known to have been armed with flintlocks.

Many of the English flintlocks of the mid-17th century had a small, pivoted metal hook fitted to the lockplate just behind the cock. From its shape it acquired the name **dog catch.** It was intended to render the pistol safe by engaging with a small notch cut into the back of the cock. Once in position, the cock was locked until the catch was manually removed. Most of the early flintlock pistols are characterized by their long, comparatively small-bore barrels. The stocks were usually plain and the butt, often oval in section, frequently had a metal band or cap at the base to prevent the wood splitting.

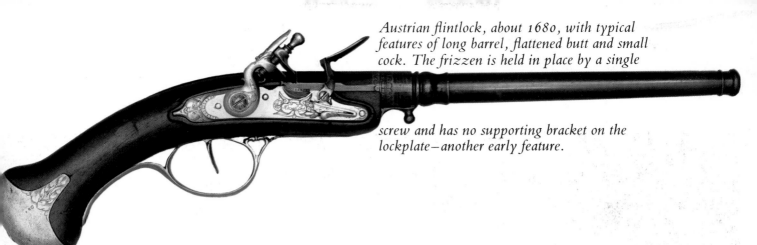

The lockplate and cock were normally of rectangular section but towards the end of the century, and during much of the 18th century, most had a flat inside surface while the outside was made concave. During the early part of the 18th century most lockplates had a rather drooping shape; this tended to become less pronounced as the century progressed.

In the interests of safety most, but not all, firearms had a trigger guard and this, together with the metal which secured the ramrod to the stock, and the cap fitted at the base of the butt, are known as the **furniture** of the firearm. On most 17th-century weapons the furniture was plain and lacking in decoration but later examples were sometimes very elaborate. The stock was usually of walnut, although other, more decorative woods were occasionally used for top-quality weapons. In America, maple was a popular substitute for walnut, particularly in the 18th and 19th century long rifles of Pennsylvania and Kentucky.

The adoption of the flintlock did not affect the system of loading and the vast majority of firearms were loaded in exactly the same way as the matchlock. A few pistols were produced in the 17th century with a barrel that could be unscrewed; powder and ball were put directly into the breech and the barrel replaced. To reduce the chances of accidental loss, the barrel was attached to the stock by a simple metal linkage. A few of the firearms of this early period were fitted with rifled barrels which gave them far higher standards of accuracy.

The blunderbuss

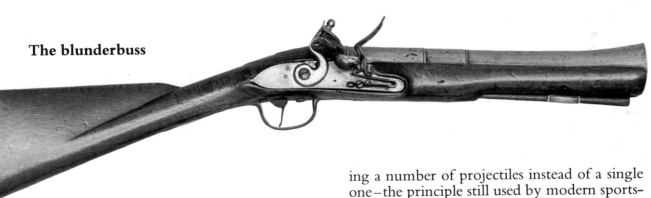

THE vast majority of early firearms were single shot—a severe limitation in an emergency when a hasty or poorly aimed shot could leave the foe unharmed and the shooter helpless. Innumerable attempts were made to overcome this restriction and a variety of complicated and often impractical devices designed to enable the same weapon to fire at least two shots from one loading. An alternative solution to the problem was to increase the chances of scoring a hit with the single shot available. One obvious way was by discharging a number of projectiles instead of a single one—the principle still used by modern sportsmen with their shotguns.

During the 17th century there emerged a popular weapon which attempted to ensure that one shot would suffice: this was the **blunderbuss.** Basically, the weapon was designed on the principle that a wide muzzle ensures a wide spread of shot. In their mistaken belief in wide barrels, gunmakers of the 17th and 18th centuries produced blunderbusses with oval barrels intended to spread the shot laterally, as well as blunderbusses with enormously belling barrels. Even a few double-

The butt of an early English blunderbuss with a brass barrel. It dates from the late 17th century and has a typical butt shape. The lock is fitted with a hook to hold the cock in a safe position — this is known as the dog-lock.

barreled blunderbusses were made. The great majority were fitted to a short stock, to be fired from the shoulder, but some smaller versions, blunderbuss pistols, were made.

Despite the basic fallacy of its design the blunderbuss did offer limited advantages and increased the chances of a hit, especially in the hands of an untrained shooter. At 40 feet most produced a shot pattern with a spread of about a two- to three-foot diameter and this obviously increased the chance of making some impact on the target. It was an easy weapon to load, taking a fair-sized charge of powder and perhaps 12–20 small lead balls. (Despite popular belief, these weapons were not loaded with old nails, stones and broken glass except in times of dire emergency.) The name blunderbuss was derived from the German *Dunderbüchse* or "thunder gun", for the flaring muzzle must have acted somewhat like a megaphone to produce a thunderous roar when it was fired.

Although a few examples of wheel-lock blunderbusses are known, the vast majority were fitted with the flintlock and date from the mid-17th century to the early part of the 19th century. Some were used by military and naval forces, but their most popular use was in the defense of home or transport; they were adopted by guards on the English mail coaches in 1784.

Many examples of the mail coach blunderbusses have survived, usually inscribed "For Her (His) Majesty's Mail Coaches" around the muzzle. It must be mentioned that not all the mail coach guards carried out their duties with the solemnity and decorum that might be desired, for among the British Post Office orders still extant are stern reminders to guards not to shoot at stray pigs and inn signs as they journeyed on their way.

In 1781, John Waters patented another very popular addition to the blunderbuss, a **bayonet.** On the blunderbuss the blade, roughly triangular in section, was pivoted near the muzzle and when folded back compressed a small V-spring. When not needed, the blade was held back against the barrel by a spring catch and if this were released, the V-spring pushed the blade quickly over so that it engaged with a small lug and locked in the forward position. The swish, click and sudden appearance of the blade were presumably a sufficient deterrent in themselves, for there seems to be no recorded occasion on which the bayonet was used for any lethal purpose. Most commonly the bayonet was fitted on the top of the barrel, but weapons with it below or at the side are well known. Many of the blunderbusses were made with brass barrels.

Very fine-quality, brass-barreled blunderbuss made by a London gunmaker — H. Mortimer, late 18th century. It has a spring-operated bayonet which is held in the position shown by the catch just behind the cock.

Pocket pistols

THE wheel-lock mechanism gave gun-makers the opportunity to produce small, portable firearms which could be managed quite well in one hand. The snaphaunce and flintlock made it even easier to construct pistols and their simplicity made it possible to produce versions smaller than ever before. Pistols of large size were fine for military use but for personal protection a very small weapon was desirable, since it was not practical to carry a large pistol at the belt or in the hand. Small firearms for personal protection are usually described as **pocket pistols.** The really miniature versions are usually called **muff-pistols,** although this term is really only one of convenience, since there is little evidence to suggest they were primarily women's weapons.

It was important that such a pistol should be as smooth as possible in outline so that it could be drawn quickly, without snagging on clothes. To this end, a specially mounted lock was devised with cock, pan and frizzen mounted centrally above the breech instead of at the side. In place of a projecting pan there was a saucer-like depression with the touch hole leading directly down into the breech. This was covered by the frizzen which was tensioned by a spring, also mounted centrally, and behind this was the cock. The whole system was known as the **box-lock.** Since the pistol was intended primarily for self-defense, range was not an important factor and the

pan was primed, the cock pulled back to the half-cock position and the frizzen closed.

To ensure maximum safety, many of these pistols were fitted with safety catches in addition to the half-cock position. The more common method was to have a sliding bar which served a double purpose. Situated above the butt, this safety catch was pushed forward and engaged with a notch at the back of the cock, thus locking it. At the same time, a forward projecting pin engaged with a corresponding hole on the frizzen, locking it shut. This double action made the weapon safe and also prevented accidental loss of the priming. With both devices it was essential to release the safety catch and pull back the cock to the full-cock position before firing. Despite their limitations, these pistols must have been popular, for many have survived.

In moments of stress, aiming was likely to be erratic and in a sudden attack in the street or on the coach there was very little time to reload a pistol. Some pocket pistols were sold in pairs, but many were made to fire at least two shots–some as many as four. With the earlier examples this was usually achieved by fitting two barrels, as on some wheel locks. These barrels were sometimes mounted jointly side by side and the pistol was either fitted with two locks, one for each barrel, or with one lock which could discharge both shots. In the latter case, the two barrels were loaded and primed and the frizzen closed. The frizzen was wide enough to cover both pans. A sliding cover blocked off one pan so that if the cock

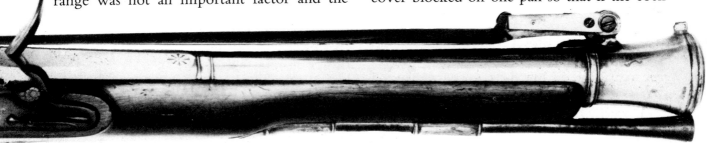

charge of powder was consequently small, as was the size of the bullet. Sights were not required or fitted.

To load the pistol, the barrel was unscrewed by means of a key. One type of key slipped over the barrel and engaged with a lug while another was inserted at the muzzle where a series of notches gave it purchase. When the barrel had been removed, powder and ball were placed directly in the breech and the barrel replaced. This system was quick and simple and obviated the need for a ramrod. When the breech had been loaded and the barrel replaced, then the

struck sparks, only one barrel fired. If the lock were now re-cocked and the sliding cover pushed clear, the second pan was exposed to the sparks.

Another method was to fit the barrels one above the other; indeed, on some pistols there were two pairs of barrels. Each barrel was fitted with its own pan and frizzen but there was only one cock, or at the most two. After normal loading and priming, the top one or two barrels could be discharged as usual. A small catch was then operated and the entire block of barrels could be manually rotated

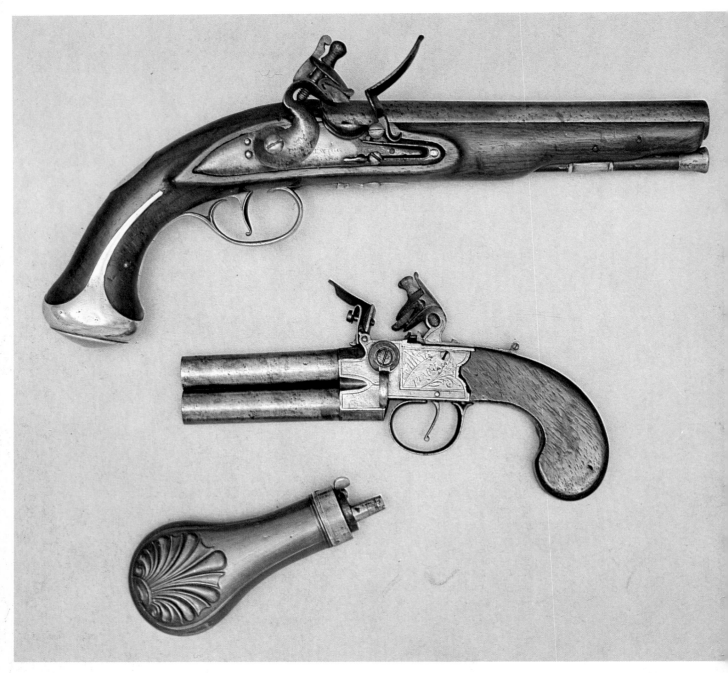

to bring the two primed, loaded but as yet unfired barrels up into position in front of the cock. Each of these could then be fired in the normal manner, giving four shots with a minimum of wasted time and effort.

Perhaps the most common method for multi-shot pistols was the tap action used on two- or three-barreled pistols. A box-lock pistol was used and the two barrels were mounted one above the other–described by collectors as **over and under.** There was only a single pan set in the breech but it was quite deep and the lower half was cut into a circular metal block. Through this block went a small hole connecting with the breech of the lower barrel.

The sequence of operation was as follows: both barrels were loaded with powder and ball and priming powder was placed in the central block. This was then rotated through 90 degrees by means of an external projection, so placing the priming inside the housing while the rim of the block now formed the floor of the pan. More priming was inserted and this top priming was connected to the breech of the top barrel. If the frizzen were now closed and the action operated, the priming flared and fired the top barrel. The block was then turned back to its original position and the first lot of priming was now in place. The frizzen was closed again, the action cocked and the lower barrel could then be fired. If the tap were left in the first position when the pistol was fully loaded, it was highly likely that both barrels would be discharged together as the flash passed through both touch holes. In the case of three-barreled pistols, the same result was achieved by turning the tap twice.

Opposite top *Brass-mounted flintlock pistol by Twigg & Bass of London, late 18th century. Its size places it between a holster pistol and a pocket pistol—many collectors describe it as an overcoat pistol.*

Center *Tap action, boxlock, flintlock pistol by Pearce. The selector ring for top or bottom barrel can be seen just below the frizzen. This type of weapon was a popular form of pocket pistol.*

Bottom *A metal powder flask of the size usually associated with pistols.*

Below *Necessary for the traveler of the 18th century and early 19th century was a pocket pistol—small enough to slip away easily but powerful enough to stop an attacker. Small pistol with concealed trigger, made by Parker of Holborn, and larger one fitted with a brass barrel and spring bayonet.*

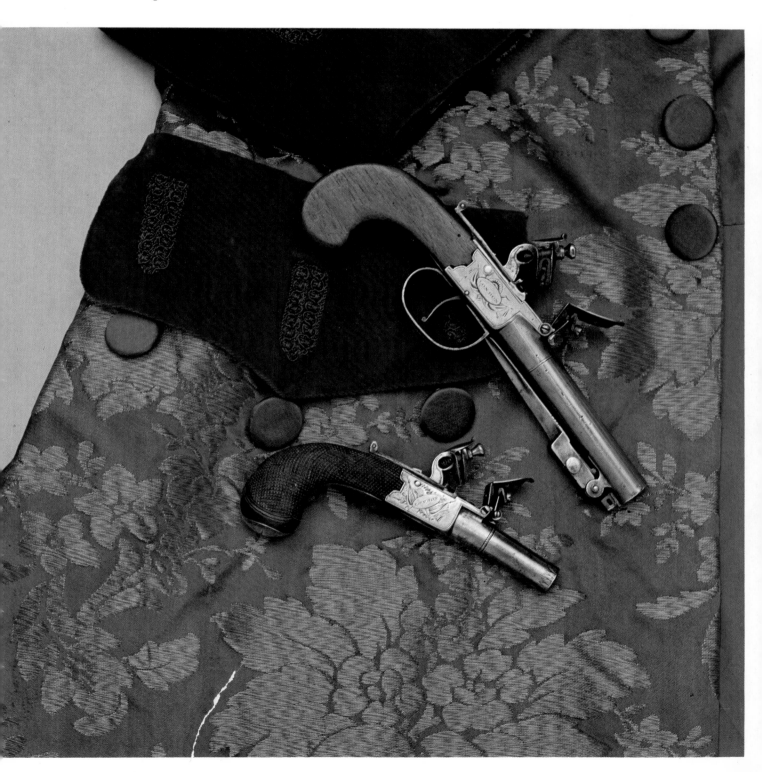

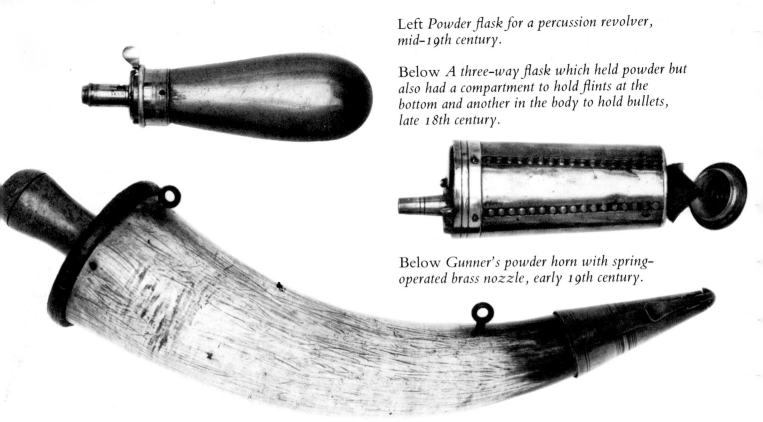

Left *Powder flask for a percussion revolver, mid-19th century.*

Below *A three-way flask which held powder but also had a compartment to hold flints at the bottom and another in the body to hold bullets, late 18th century.*

Below *Gunner's powder horn with spring-operated brass nozzle, early 19th century.*

Powder flasks

A readily available supply of powder in some safe but convenient container was obviously essential for every shooter. At an early date, probably in the early 15th century, the **powder horn** or **powder flask** evolved. At first, it was fairly crude and any suitable receptacle–from a horn to a seed-gourd–might be used. Pourers were at first simple, but as techniques improved so did design and by the early 16th century most powder flasks had a tapered, metal pouring tube at one end of the flask. No doubt the earliest examples of the tube were closed by a bung or cork, but in the 16th century a simple, spring-operated cover was being used and soon this was developed so that the flask delivered a carefully measured amount of powder. The nozzle was fitted with two **cut-offs,** or metal discs, one at the base and one at the nozzle. Methods of operation varied slightly, but on most the flask was inverted so that powder ran into the pourer. The bottom cut-off was then operated, so closing off the pourer from the main body of the flask. If the second cut-off were now opened, the charge of powder could be poured into the barrel.

Cow horns were ideal for the construction of flasks, since they were light, waterproof and readily available. The horn was boiled, then flattened until it was roughly rectangular in section. After being allowed to cool and harden, one end was permanently sealed by a wooden block while the point was cut off and another block with the pourer fitted into place. Often these horns of the late 16th and 17th centuries were decorated with simple, incised pictures, usually hunting scenes. More elaborate flasks were made from Y-shaped pieces of antler, often finely decorated with carving in high relief. Some were made in annular form, beautifully inlaid, others were fashioned from tortoise shell and gourds.

In the 18th century, metal largely replaced the other materials. On some flasks the metal was left plain, while on others it was covered with material. Some, known as three-way flasks, were more elaborate, for besides functioning as powder flasks they were also designed to hold spare flints in the base and a number of bullets in an internal compartment. During the 19th century very large quantities of metal, pear-shaped or tear-shaped flasks were produced, often with the pourer, or charger, graded so that it could be adjusted to give a variety of different-sized charges. As metal-working skills developed, many of these flasks were embossed with hunting or martial scenes, medallions and any number of other fancies. Copper and brass were most often used but a few special ones were of silver, while brittania metal and pewter were occasionally employed.

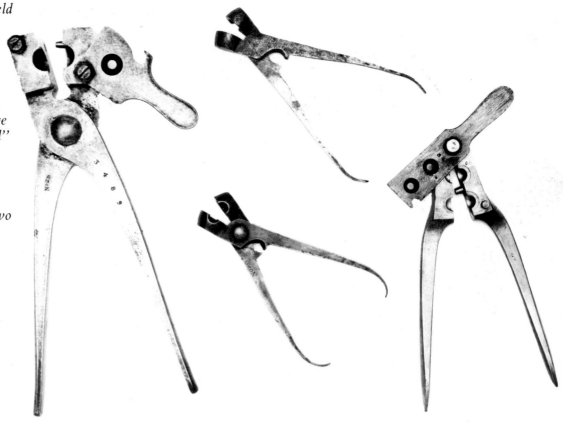

Right *Mold for Enfield rifle casting a single bullet .577 ins. diameter.*

Center *Two scissors molds for pistol balls—note the sharpened edge for cutting off the "tail" of the bullet.*

Far right *Mold for percussion Adams revolver which casts two bullets—this one has a pivoted cutter.*

Bullet molds

EQUALLY as important as a powder supply was a supply of bullets. Although these could be purchased in bulk, it behoved the prudent shooter to have his own means of production. At some early date, probably during the 14th century, lead, an easily cast material, was found to be a very suitable metal for bullets. By the late 14th century references to ladles and molds are to be found. The method of casting bullets altered little over the centuries: first the lead is melted (it is important that it be neither too hot nor too cold). Some of the molten lead is removed from the crucible by means of a ladle and this is poured carefully into a mold and allowed to cool. The pouring has to be steady and slow so that there are no trapped air bubbles. The form of the earliest molds is unknown. Possibly they were of stone, but by the 16th century brass and iron were being used. These early molds were of the type called "gang molds"—that is, they cast several bullets at one time. The mold consisted of two or more long, thin metal plates with appropriately sized and shaped recesses. For convenience, the plates were fitted with long handles and the tops of the leaves were beveled so that when closed, a trough was formed for the lead to flow along and so into the hole leading to the actual recess.

During the 17th century most molds were simplified and the arms made much thinner. At the same time the first scissor molds appeared—these had two arms pivoted near one end at which was a block of metal cut with the appropriate cavity. (The cavity was formed either by hamering the metal around a hard core or, as on later examples, by using a bulbous cherry bit which was rotated to grind out the cavity.) When the two halves were brought together, molten lead was poured in through a small hole at the top and when the ball was set the two arms were opened and the ball fell out. During the process a small tail of lead, the **sprue,** was formed by the lead which filled the channel leading into the cavity, and this had to be cut off. Many of the scissor molds had two sharpened edges near the point of the pivot and these were used to clip off the sprue; a number of 18th century molds had a flat plate pivoted on the cavity block which served the same purpose. The plate was made with a hole in it leading directly to the bullet cavity, forming the top plate of the mold. When the lead had cooled, the plate was moved forward and effectively cut off the sprue.

In the 19th century many molds were made with a variety of removable plugs which could be inserted into the cavity to produce hollow noses or bases in the cast bullets. During that time machines were designed to mass produce better quality bullets than those cast by hand.

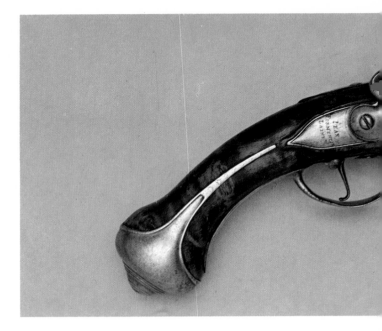

French firearms

MOST of those matchlocks known to have been made in France have a characteristic, sharp curve to the butt which gives them a hook-like shape. This form was usually described as a **petronel,** derived from a word meaning "chest", and for this reason it is thought that such weapons were fired with the butt held against the chest. This seems a very awkward position and one which would seem to preclude any form of aiming, although many matchlocks were fitted with rear sights.

Most wheel-locks, except those made in France, had their mainspring attached to the inside of the lockplate. On French wheel-locks the mainspring was separate and secured to the inside of the stock. Although this in no way affected the action of the mechanism, it somewhat weakened the stock since more wood had to be cut out to accommodate the mainspring. French wheel-lock pistols and guns have a rather characteristic shape, for the wheel was usually large and required, in consequence, a large plate which meant that the stock was widened to accommodate it. At the turn of the 16th century, French butts were usually far slimmer than those on German pistols with their large ball butts, and had an egg-shaped pommel which was often gracefully fluted or faceted.

The firearms industry was greatly helped by the interest of King Louis XIII (1610–1642). Like most monarchs, Louis was a keen hunter but he had a deeper, genuine interest in firearms themselves and made a collection. Fortunately for posterity, in 1673 his successor, Louis XIV, ordered a complete list of the collection to be made. An inventory number was allocated to each weapon and this number was stamped on the stock of the weapon; it is thus still possible to identify items from the collection.

It was during the reign of Louis XIII that the flintlock was introduced by Marin Le Bourgeoys. At first it was used only on French weapons, but its obvious advantage soon ensured its wider adoption. Most of the earliest examples of French flintlocks are, in fact, found on long arms, particularly sporting arms. Pistols with the new system of ignition seem to have been made only from about 1630 and all have very long barrels, designed to ensure strength at the breech. The stocks were straight and the butt often oval in section with a flattened "fishtail"

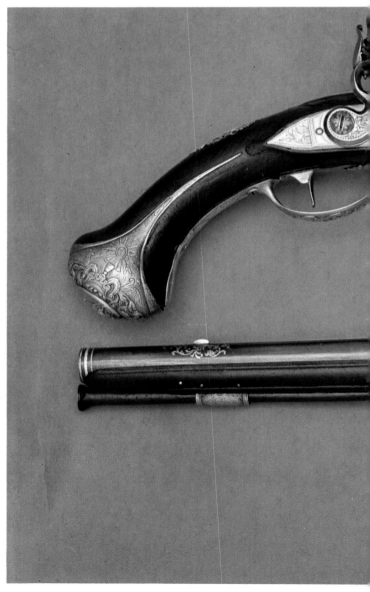

Bottom *A pair of very fine flintlock pistols by Chasteau of Paris with the barrels blued and gilded. The long spurs and general shape suggest that they date from the late 17th or early 18th century. They were a present to Duke Charles August, who held land on the Rhine.*

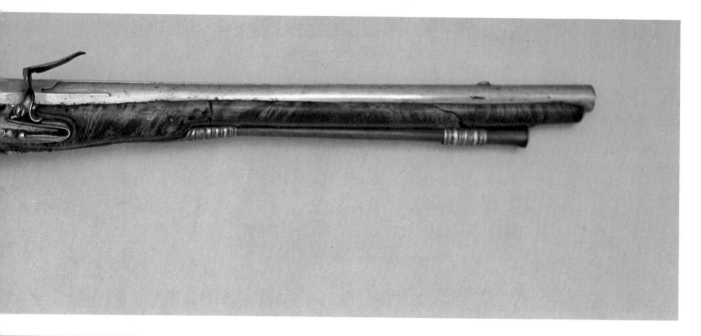

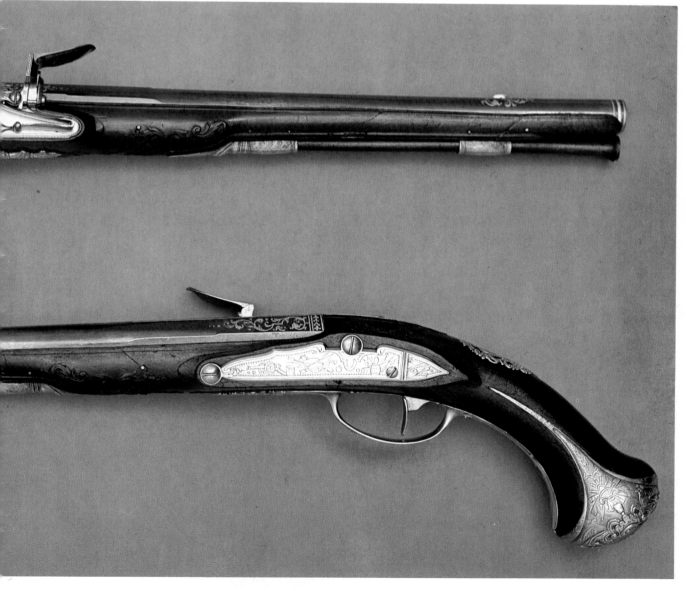

end which was tipped with a decorative, embossed or chiseled metal cap.

During the 18th century, and particularly under Napoleon, the French firearms industry flourished and expanded. In addition to the makers based in Paris, arsenals were developed at Saint-Étienne, Charleville and Souillac, the majority of their output being military. **Charleville** was made the first Royal Manufactory in France and its name is often used to describe the infantry musket introduced in 1762, although the weapon was also produced in other armories.

There was a demand from the aristocracy for decorated sporting guns but with the Revolution this market dried up and was replaced by a larger demand for simple, military weapons. Following the chaos of the late 1780s and 1790s, a new moneyed class arose and a new demand for good-quality weapons grew up. One name stands out from among the French makers-that of Boutet. Nicolas-Noël Boutet was one of the King's gunmakers fortunate enough to survive the upheaval and in 1792 he was made director of a new government factory set up at Versailles. Although primarily for standard military weapons, it also produced a number of special, high-quality weapons. The decoration on these was elaborate and of superb quality, incorporating inlay of silver or steel, carving of the stock and blueing and gilding on the barrels. A number of important presentation sets or garnitures of arms were produced. These usually comprised a pair of pistols and one or more long arms, perhaps a rifle or a carbine. These were fitted into a case and decorated *en suite*. The pistol butt was usually sharply angled, forming almost a right angle to the stock.

Spanish firearms

DURING the Middle Ages, certain towns in Spain had gained a wide reputation for the quality of their sword blades. This ability to work metal stood the armorers in good stead when firearms appeared in the Iberian peninsula. The earliest recorded mention of firearms in Spain is in 1342, and by the mid-16th century a firearms industry was flourishing in Madrid. Spanish wheel-locks were made and in general, are remarkable for their plainness.

Most characteristic Spanish flintlocks were fitted with a type of lock known as the **miguelet,** of which there were a number of variations. In many ways the miguelet lock resembled the early Scandinavian snaplock, but whether it was in fact a variation or was developed separately, is not clear. The most common type had a characteristic appearance with a frizzen which was rather short and square with the face of the steel vertically grooved. The jaws which held the flint were rather large and rectangular, unlike the oval shape usual on French flintlocks. A large screw passed through the top jaw and engaged with the lower section. Since the mainspring on these weapons was often very strong, the gunmaker felt bound to give the shooter something which would afford a good grip. To this end, most Spanish firearms had either a pivoted bar or else a large ring fitted at the top of the screw securing the jaws. The internal mechanism of the miguelet differed from that of the French lock and also resembled the Scandinavian one. There were two sears, one for half and one for full cock, and both passed through the lockplate and engaged with the cock. For safe carrying, the half-cock sear had a deep notch which received the toe of the cock and held it securely even when the trigger was pressed. If the cock was pulled further back, the toe engaged with the full-cock sear which had no notch and the action of the trigger pulled this and the half-cock sear back through the lockplate, so allowing the cock to fly forward and strike sparks. Another feature of the miguelet was the fitting of the mainspring on the outside of the lockplate; the end pressed directly on the heel of the cock.

In addition to the firearm center at Madrid, another flourished in Ripoll, a town in Catalonia in eastern Spain, producing weapons of quality and distinctive appearance. It seems that the individual gunsmiths of Madrid produced the whole weapon, whereas in Ripoll there was specialization, with different craftsmen producing locks, stocks or barrels.

Spanish gunmakers were particularly skilled in the manufacture of gun barrels. Not only were these barrels technically sound, but they, were frequently decorated and dated. The barrel makers and lockmakers of Spain were justly proud of their products and put their name and mark to them. Spanish barrels were so highly regarded, particularly by sportsmen, that they were often purchased by foreigners who then had them mounted in their own stocks. Long arms made in Spain often have a very characteristic fluting on

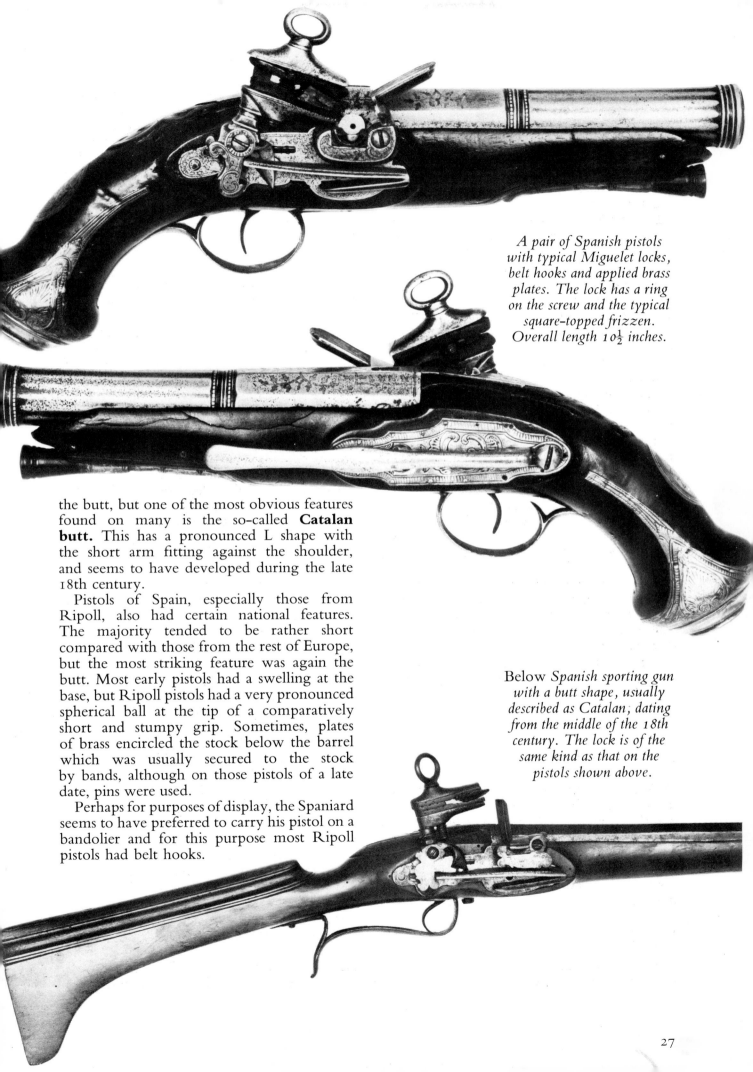

A pair of Spanish pistols with typical Miguelet locks, belt hooks and applied brass plates. The lock has a ring on the screw and the typical square-topped frizzen. Overall length 10½ inches.

the butt, but one of the most obvious features found on many is the so-called **Catalan butt.** This has a pronounced L shape with the short arm fitting against the shoulder, and seems to have developed during the late 18th century.

Pistols of Spain, especially those from Ripoll, also had certain national features. The majority tended to be rather short compared with those from the rest of Europe, but the most striking feature was again the butt. Most early pistols had a swelling at the base, but Ripoll pistols had a very pronounced spherical ball at the tip of a comparatively short and stumpy grip. Sometimes, plates of brass encircled the stock below the barrel which was usually secured to the stock by bands, although on those pistols of a late date, pins were used.

Perhaps for purposes of display, the Spaniard seems to have preferred to carry his pistol on a bandolier and for this purpose most Ripoll pistols had belt hooks.

Below Spanish sporting gun with a butt shape, usually described as Catalan, dating from the middle of the 18th century. The lock is of the same kind as that on the pistols shown above.

Flintlock pistol of the early 18th century with a barrel marked "Lazarino". This may mean that the barrel was made by a member of the famous

Italian Cominazzo family, but the name was often fraudulently added by other makers in order to sell their products.

Other European firearms

BY the mid-16th century, most countries had some firearms industry at work, although it is not possible in many cases to identify pieces as being from one particular area. Spain had a flourishing gun trade, as did France, but Italy seems to have lagged behind somewhat–although in one or two places good-quality work was carried out. Brescia, in the north, was noted throughout most of the 18th century for the very high standard of its metal work. During the late 17th century the Brescians produced a number of pistols with all-metal stocks. They were famous for their chiseled decoration on firearms, as were some other makers working in Florence and Bargi (near Bologna). From the area near Brescia came the Cominazzo family of barrel makers. The family is known to have been in the trade since the mid-16th century and continued in it until the mid-19th, although their greatest triumphs date from the 17th century. So well known were their names that it was not uncommon for other makers to stamp their own inferior barrels with the name Cominazzo.

Belgium developed an arms industry during the 16th century which seems to have had its center at Liège. The gunmakers grew more organized and by the 17th century are known to have had a system of proving–testing the quality of–their firearms. During the late 18th and early 19th century, Liège turned out large quantities of cheap, plain, but serviceable flintlocks. But later the term "Belgian made" in the firearms industry came to stand for shoddy workmanship.

From the area near the Polish-Czechoslovakian border came that very delicate and attractive gun known as the tschinke. This is most commonly found with a wheel-lock fitted, but some using flintlocks were made.

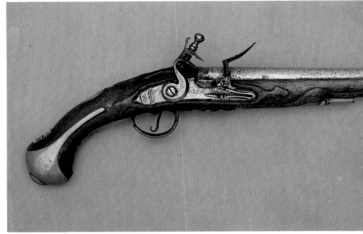

Above Prussian flintlock pistol of mid-18th century bearing on the lock plate "Potsdam Magaz".

Below Finely decorated pair of flintlock pistols by Hess of Zweibrücken. The furniture is gilded and the barrels are blued and gilded with the locks polished bright.

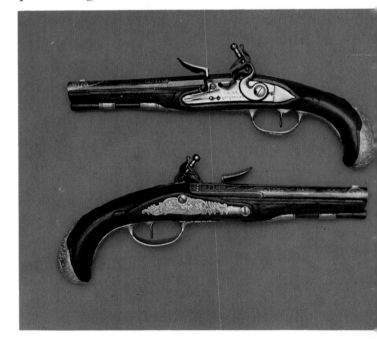

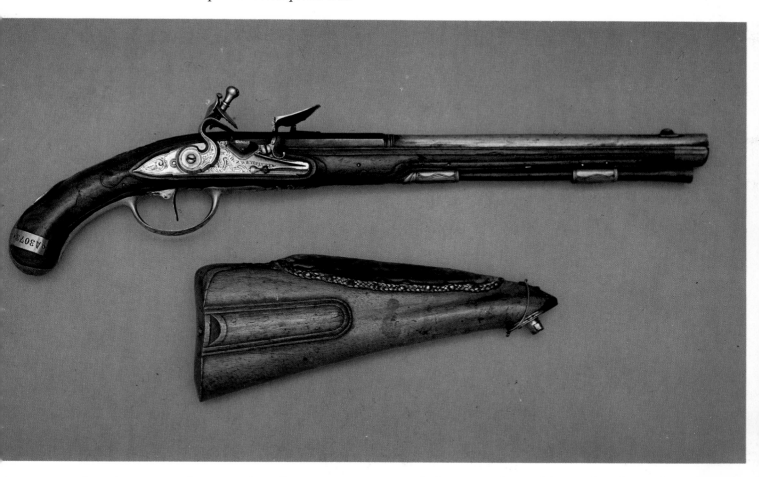

Austrian gunmakers continued to manufacture wheel-locks much later than elsewhere in Europe and may well have continued right through the 18th century.

In the town of Regensburg, in present Bavaria, there was established a family of gunmakers who dominated the arms trade. The first of them, Georg Kuchenreuter, arrived there in the 1620s and his descendants were to continue working there until this century.

During the 17th century, Holland became one of the main supply sources of firearms for Europe. Many of the wheel-lock pistols used by the two sides during the English Civil Wars (1642–48) were of Dutch origin. The Dutch form of the snaphaunce was to remain in use in North Africa until early this century and is still found on some weapons there today. One remarkable group of Dutch pistols was of superb quality, with stocks of ivory and beautifully carved butts.

The Dutch style of firearm mechanism seems to have influenced Russian design during the 17th century, although the stocks were more individualistic with long butts which were held, not to the shoulder, but to the cheek. Decoration was lavish, even if not of very delicate workmanship, and reflects the Asiatic influences on Russian art. Peter the Great, Czar from 1672–1725, was determined to bring Russia more in line with Western development and among his numerous reforms was the setting up of a national arsenal. He chose Tula, lying to the south of Moscow, a town noted for its iron and steel production. The arsenal was officially opened in 1705 and employed nearly 3,000 workmen, mostly engaged in producing military weapons, although some special weapons were made for the Imperial court. Peter employed a number of foreign craftsmen to work at Tula and these included Swedes, Danes and Germans. The basic style of the Russian arms from Tula was French, for the craftsmen relied heavily for inspiration on a book of designs by Nicholas Guérard, published in Paris. In the early 19th century, an Englishman was employed to take charge of the mechanical workshop, but much of the work was undertaken at home by the workmen and, presumably, finished at the arsenal. Some weapons were made in St Petersburg, now called Leningrad.

The blunderbuss was popular in Poland and Russia while the rest of Europe, apart from Britain, never greatly valued this firearm.

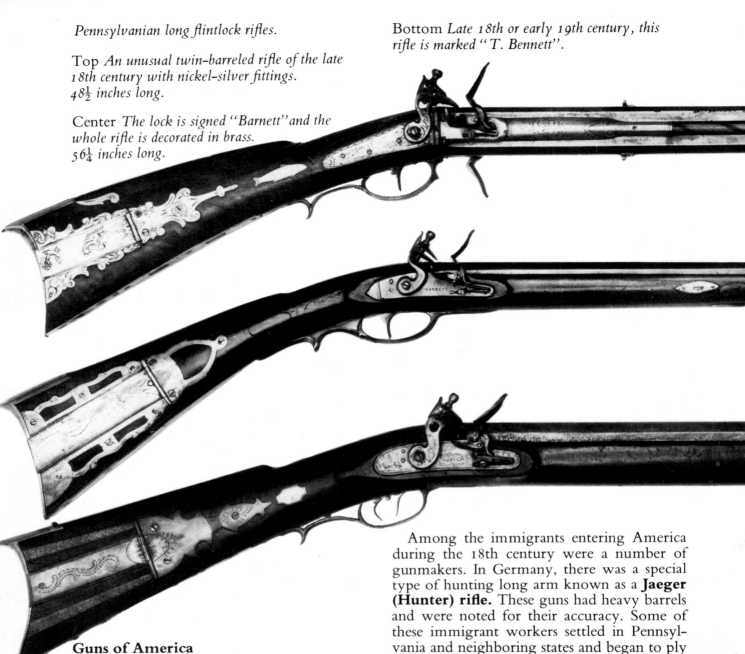

Pennsylvanian long flintlock rifles.

Top *An unusual twin-barreled rifle of the late 18th century with nickel-silver fittings. $48\frac{1}{2}$ inches long.*

Center *The lock is signed "Barnett" and the whole rifle is decorated in brass. $56\frac{1}{4}$ inches long.*

Bottom *Late 18th or early 19th century, this rifle is marked "T. Bennett".*

Guns of America

IN the early days of its history, when the continent of North America was an area explored and disputed over by the Dutch, French, Spanish, Portuguese and British, each national group imported its own firearms. It was not until settled communities began to develop that anything approaching a native gunmaking industry arose. Its growth was greatly accelerated by the American Revolution (1776–1783) when the supply of arms from Britain abruptly ceased. Local Committees of Safety were set up and these ordered weapons for their militia, usually drawing up clear specifications for the pattern. Most of the first production models were based on the British Brown Bess musket, or the French infantry musket. Since raw materials and facilities were limited, many of these so-called Committee of Safety muskets were fairly simple but, nonetheless, effective.

Among the immigrants entering America during the 18th century were a number of gunmakers. In Germany, there was a special type of hunting long arm known as a **Jaeger (Hunter) rifle.** These guns had heavy barrels and were noted for their accuracy. Some of these immigrant workers settled in Pennsylvania and neighboring states and began to ply their trade. As a result of their changed circumstances and environment they began, perhaps unconsciously, to modify the Jaeger and from these changes evolved the famous **Pennsylvania long rifle**, also known as the **Kentucky rifle.** It had a long, octagonal rifled barrel and fired a fairly small-bore bullet, but it had range and accuracy, as many British officers found to their cost during the war. The butt was long and had a graceful droop with a deeply concave cut at the back so that it sat firmly and comfortably against the shoulder. Decoration was usually of brass and a cavity cut into the butt was covered by a hinged lid of brass. Into the cavity went the waxed patches which were wrapped around the bullet before it was loaded. Brass was also used to decorate the stock, which was normally fashioned from maple. A few pistols were also made by the craftsmen who produced the rifles, but these were far less plentiful.

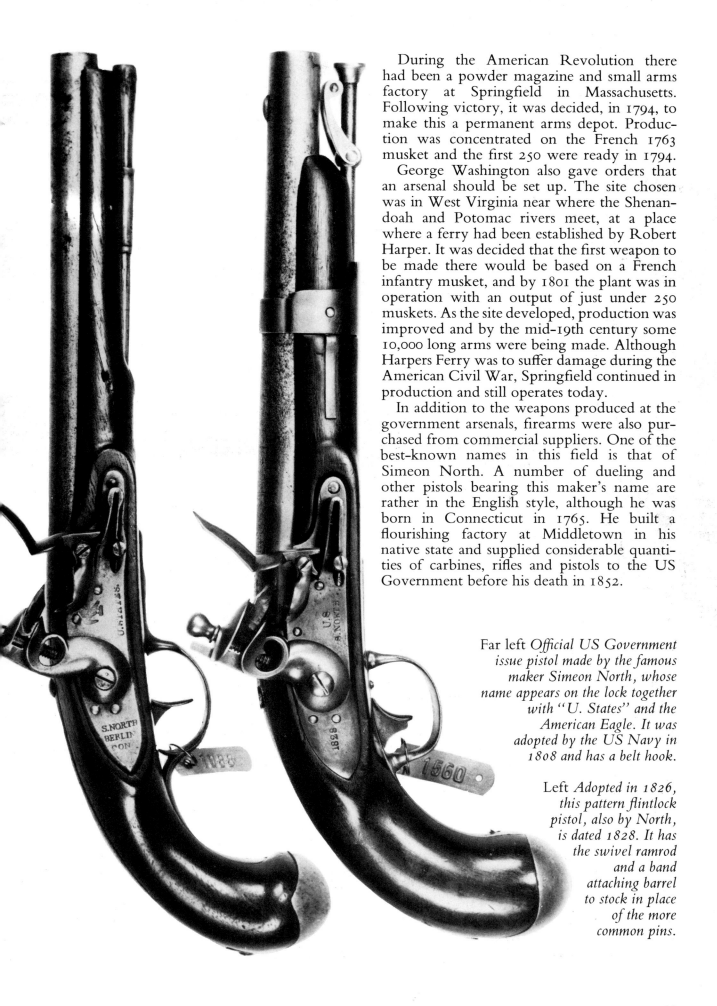

During the American Revolution there had been a powder magazine and small arms factory at Springfield in Massachusetts. Following victory, it was decided, in 1794, to make this a permanent arms depot. Production was concentrated on the French 1763 musket and the first 250 were ready in 1794.

George Washington also gave orders that an arsenal should be set up. The site chosen was in West Virginia near where the Shenandoah and Potomac rivers meet, at a place where a ferry had been established by Robert Harper. It was decided that the first weapon to be made there would be based on a French infantry musket, and by 1801 the plant was in operation with an output of just under 250 muskets. As the site developed, production was improved and by the mid-19th century some 10,000 long arms were being made. Although Harpers Ferry was to suffer damage during the American Civil War, Springfield continued in production and still operates today.

In addition to the weapons produced at the government arsenals, firearms were also purchased from commercial suppliers. One of the best-known names in this field is that of Simeon North. A number of dueling and other pistols bearing this maker's name are rather in the English style, although he was born in Connecticut in 1765. He built a flourishing factory at Middletown in his native state and supplied considerable quantities of carbines, rifles and pistols to the US Government before his death in 1852.

Far left *Official US Government issue pistol made by the famous maker Simeon North, whose name appears on the lock together with "U. States" and the American Eagle. It was adopted by the US Navy in 1808 and has a belt hook.*

Left *Adopted in 1826, this pattern flintlock pistol, also by North, is dated 1828. It has the swivel ramrod and a band attaching barrel to stock in place of the more common pins.*

31

Flintlock pistol which exhibits many features of Balkan and Turkish pistols. There is no ramrod, although one is simulated.

In general appearance the pistol is reminiscent of a late 17th century weapon, but in fact is very much later.

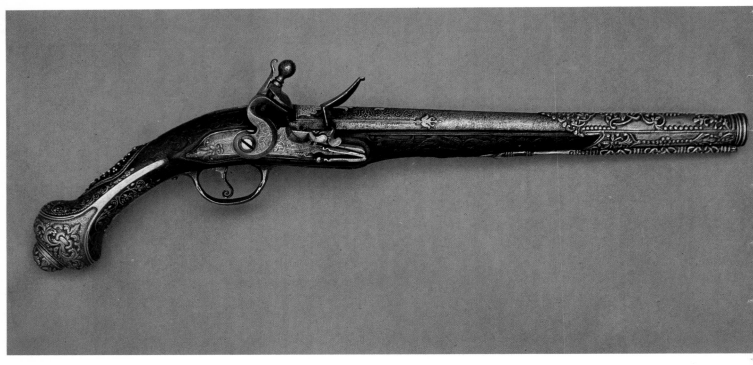

Balkan firearms

IN the area of Europe closely associated with Turkey and the Near East—namely Albania, Greece, Yugoslavia—commonly called the Balkans, a rather special type of pistol developed. In most cases the workmanship was rather indifferent but the decoration was lavish. Most were flintlocks with a French-type lock and a stock reminiscent of the late 17th or early 18th century European pistols—long and slender, but with a fairly prominent ball pommel. The furniture was of brass, steel or cast silver The stock and barrel were bound with wire or plates of embossed brass or white metal. Similar forms of decoration were applied to the butt, too, and many of the more expensive specimens were inset with semi-precious stones, pieces of coral or minerals. On some pistols there are to be found various marks and inscriptions, many of which are spurious attempts to copy those found on western examples.

A few really good-quality pieces are to be found, but of these the majority were made for the purpose of export or to be given as gifts to persons of importance. One form common during the 18th and 19th centuries is known as the **rat-tail**, for it was a particularly thin form with the butt in very nearly the same line as the stock and with an onion-shaped pommel with a small finial. Many of the Balkan pistols had no ramrod fitted into the stock, for it was a separate item carried on a cord.

Asiatic firearms

BEFORE the advent of European traders, the Chinese and Arabs seem to have had some form of crude firearm, but details of these are vague. When the Portuguese first reached India, they took with them the matchlock, which was to remain in use until early this century. The shape varied, but most were long with a very simple stock and a butt which was straight and without embellishment. The serpentine mechanism was fitted inside the stock, unlike that of Europe which was in the form of a separate lock. Triggers were often fashioned into elaborate shapes.

The flintlock was also used extensively in India, both on pistols and on longarms which had a variety of stocks. One of the most distinctive forms is the **Afghan** or **Scinde stock**, which has a strongly curved, almost semi-circular butt. On both forms of arms, barrels were secured to the stock by a series of bands, usually of leather or brass. The East India Company played an important part in the development of India. Among their imports was the British-made **gun lock** and these locks are often to be found on muskets. The locks bear the Company's mark: either a heart shape enclosing the letters "E V I C", or a rampant lion holding a ball.

Japan also favored the matchlock; such matchlocks usuably have short and very heavy barrels with brass springs and fittings and some inlay on the stock.

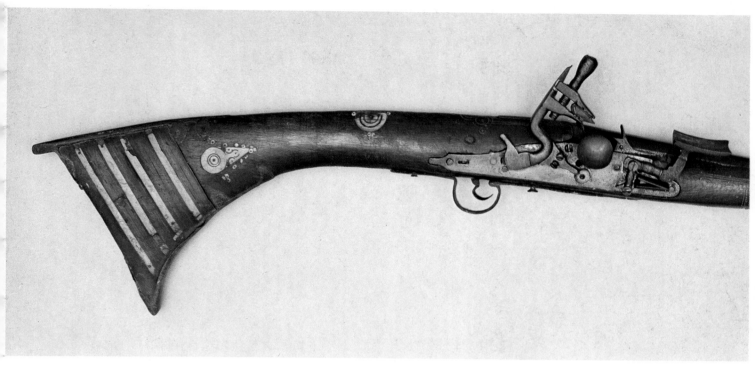

The manufacture of firearms

IN the early days of firearms, the gunmaker was little more than a smith who cast barrels or fashioned them from metal strips and hoops. The stocks were simply planks or metal bars, but with the advent of the wheel-lock the craft became far more complex. A top-quality wheel-lock involved the skills of several craftsmen and artistes, each of whom might sign his name on the relevant part. Barrel maker, stock maker and lock maker all would have contributed and they might well have worked to designs drawn up by an artist.

Barrel makers in the early days produced a rectangular plate of metal which was then wrapped around a former and hammered and welded into a tube. This was then bored and finished and the breech end closed with a plug. In many cases, the barrel might well be treated by a controlled rusting process to give it a beautiful brown finish. The lock called for a number of separate parts which had to be made, assembled and fitted so that they functioned with certainty and precision. These jobs required the services of a skilled smith for the actual production, with the help of an apprentice for the smoothing and fitting, but the finishing and final fitting was left, to another skilled man. The stock, normally of walnut, called for a high degree of skill in the shaping, whether intended for a pistol or long arm. The barrel, trigger guard, butt cap,

ramrod pipes and lock all had to be set into the wood with a neat fit and a minimum amount of cutting of the wood which might weaken the stock.

Once the entire firearm had been assembled, it was then stripped down for the final finishing, trimming, adjusting, polishing and decoration. Lock parts were polished and hardened and probably engraved with the maker's name, which might also be inscribed on the barrel. Many 18th century English pistols were decorated with inlaid silver wire in the form of curls and scrolls and this called for the cutting of a narrow channel into the stock. Into this was laid the silver wire, which was then hammered gently to spread it and make it grip and hold in place. Silver furniture such as the butt cap was normally cast, presumably in quantity, and fitted as required. For cased weapons there were extra items such as powder flasks, bullet molds, screw-drivers, spare rods and other optional pieces. Many of these were supplied in bulk from the workshops of Birmingham.

Barrels were tested before being sold; this process was known as proving and took the form of exploding a larger than normal charge in the breech. If, after this proving and a visual examination, no flaw was found, the barrel was then stamped to show that it was of the required standard. Most manufacturing centers, such as Liège, Paris, London, Birmingham and Amsterdam, had their own recognized symbol or proof mark.

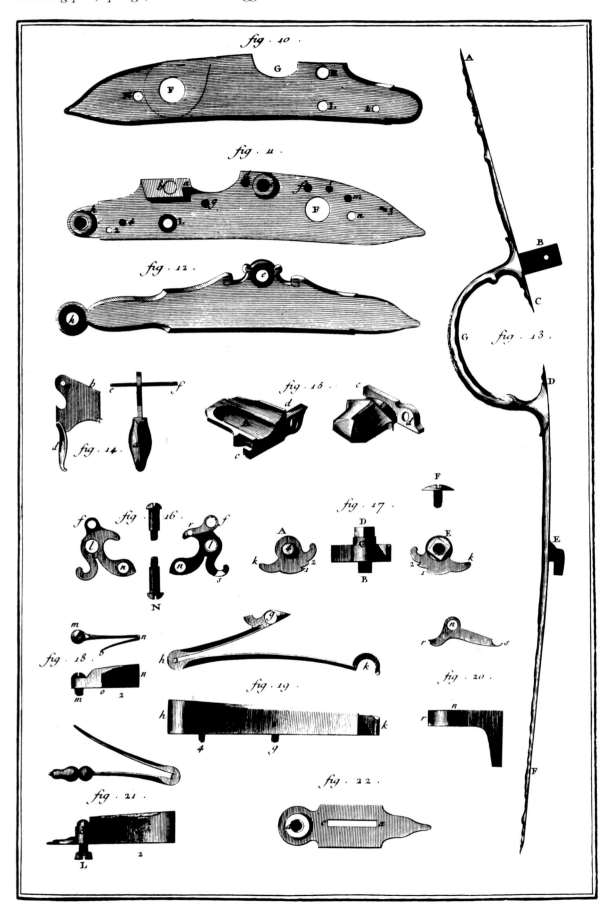

A selection of the many tools required by the gunmaker of the mid–18th century. It includes various gauges, clamps and screw-cutting tools.

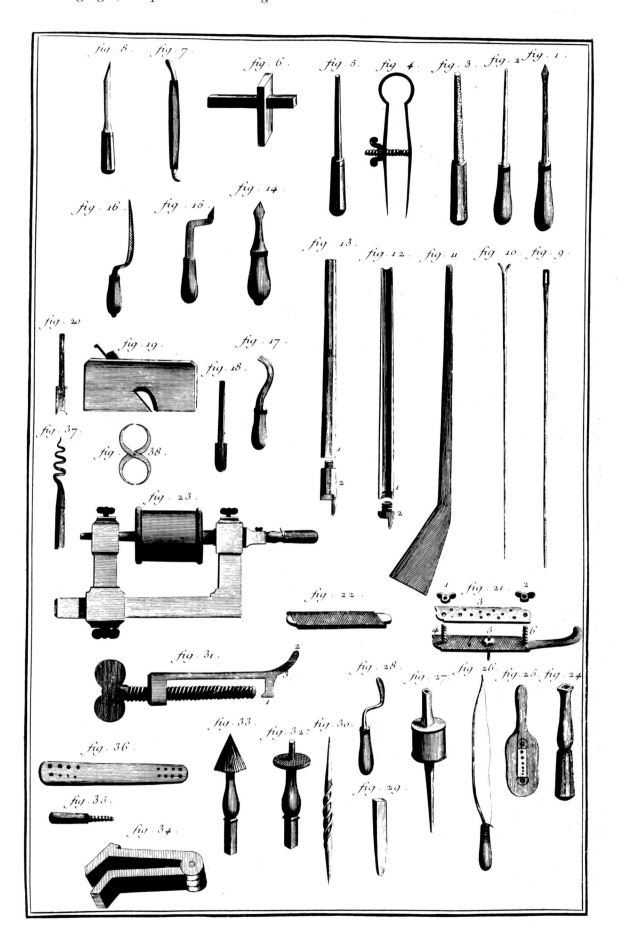

Dueling

IN the past, "honor" to the male was a peculiarly precious virtue, not to be lost without a struggle. Unfortunately, to many of the nobility the dangers of losing it were manifold: an insult, real or imagined, called for a challenge which was followed by an apology or, if this was refused, a duel. Before the advent of gunpowder, duels were settled by combat using some form of edged weapon, but firearms were soon called on to settle these futile, murderous encounters. At first, any pair of pistols were used. Later, towards the end of the 18th century, a specialized weapon was developed. Its design was obviously dictated by the ritual of the duel but essentially the **dueling pistol** was a precise, plain, reliable, easy-to-aim pistol. In most duels there was little enough time to stand and take careful aim, for most dueling codes merely stated that the command to fire was to be given and it was then up to the participants: he who shot first and accurately might well live to kill another day.

Codes of dueling were drawn up in the late 18th century which, like all codified systems, were modified and elaborated. One

form was when both combatants equidistant from a fixed point faced one another and fired at a signal, but other forms were used, such as one where the two opponents moved towards each other, passing one another and firing within a set time limit. Each of the opponents had an assistant known as his second, one of whose duties was to inspect the weapons and satisfy himself that they were of acceptable condition and make.

Dueling pistols
The first specialized weapons appeared about 1770–80, a period when the sword was losing its dominance. The dueling pistol was usually fitted with a heavy, octagonal barrel and fired a comparatively small bullet. Sights were invariably fitted. Since the flight of the bullet was obviously affected by any number of factors, many of these weapons had a special ramrod for loading. At one end could be screwed a small cylinder to hold the charge of powder. This was held vertically and the pistol barrel lowered over it. The pistol and ramrod were then rotated through 180°, so depositing the powder directly into the breach. This ensured that no grains were lost by sticking on the inside of the barrel.

The stock was usually plain, lacking any decoration apart from the butt cap found on some pistols. To ensure a firm grip the trigger guard, from early in the 19th century, was fitted with a downward curving appendage at the rear. This spur was shaped to afford a good grip by the second finger. The spur, together with the shape of the butt, was planned so that the pistol came, more or less automatically, into the correct aiming position as soon as the arm was raised. Some dueling pistols were fitted with a hair trigger, which meant that absolutely minimum pressure had to be applied to fire the pistol. To display fairness and afford equal opportunities for both contestants, most dueling pistols were supplied cased and in pairs.

Opposite *Cruikshank's cartoon depicts dueling in a far less glamorous light than was usual at the time. Dueling was a persistent drain on life in France, but in Britain was less common — although indulged in by many famous people such as the Duke of Wellington.*

Below top *Fine quality dueling pistol, made by A. Key of St Andrews, Scotland, early 19th century. It is half-stocked with a hook butt with fine cross hatching. The trigger pull required to activate the lock can be adjusted by the screw set just in front of the trigger.*

Bottom *Large, double-barreled pistol by a very famous London gunmaker, Durs Egg. There are two triggers and two locks.*

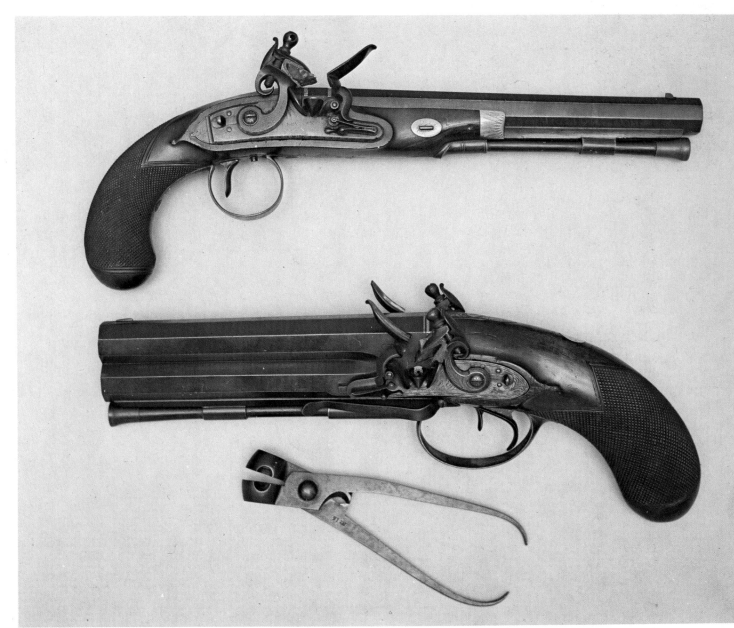

Scottish pistols with curly ramshorn butts. Both retain their ramrods and belt hooks. The steel work is engraved and the two small ovals set into

the butts bear the name "G. DOWNE" and the date 1781. These pistols were made by I. Murdoch.

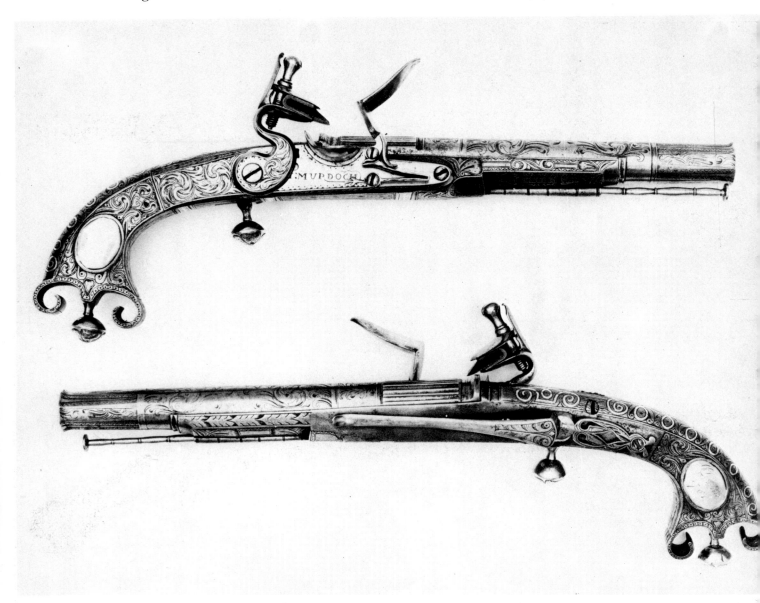

Scottish pistols

SCOTLAND, with its belligerent lairds and close clan loyalties, was a fertile ground for continuous combat and incipient hostility often flared into open warfare. There was, too, a more or less constant state of war with England. To the clansman, weapons were a normal part of dress: in addition to a broad sword he often carried a pistol and these were to develop a number of special features peculiar to Scotland.

Early examples of Scottish pistols are usually long and when found in pairs are distinctive in that one pistol has a conventional right-hand lock while the second has the lock fitted on the left. Like so many Spanish pistols, many of those from Scotland have belt hooks. Most of the early Scottish pistols

have snaphaunce locks of a characteristic construction with the pan cover connected by a rod to the tumbler, so that it would open just before the steel was struck by the flint. This type of lock had no safety or half-cock position: the sear passed through the lockplate to engage directly on the tip of the cock, but later models had the sear engaging internally with the tumbler. Other characteristics of this early pistol are the fishtail-shaped butt with curling tips and the some-what pear-shaped trigger which lacks a guard.

Surviving examples of these early pistols are rare; the more common form developed toward the latter part of the 17th century and this used a combined steel and pan cover, as in the normal flintlock. The butt of this later type was not rounded but of rectangular section–known by collectors as **slab-sided.**

Below *Late 17th century, Scottish, all-metal pistol. The ball trigger and heart-shaped pommel to the butt were common features of these weapons.*

The pistol was fitted with a long, thin belt hook.

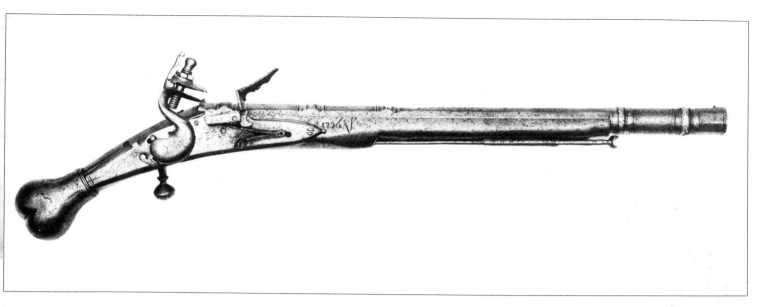

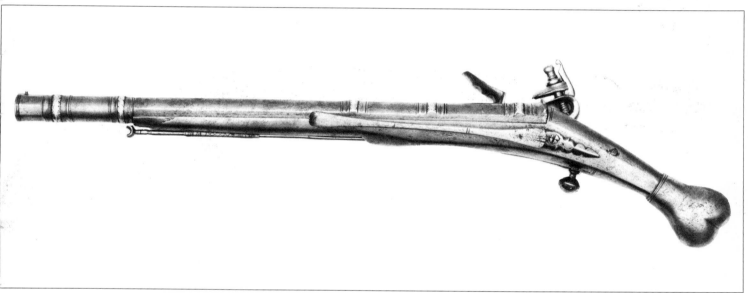

Scottish firearms

Most Scottish pistols are described as **ramshorn** because of the shape of the butt, with its two inward curling scrolls. Between these scrolls was a ball which could be unscrewed, and into this ball was fitted a long, narrow spike, which was used to clear the touch holes of corrosion. Simpler versions of the ramshorn variety were later issued to some Scottish troops up until 1795. These had a simple heart shape which merely hinted at the older, elaborate scrolls. Most of the 18th and 19th century pistols produced had metal stocks and a barrel which was ridged longitudinally at the breech. The ramrods, now made of metal, were very thin with a small disc at the end. During the 19th century there was a romantic revival of interest in all things Scottish and as a result of this revival some very elaborately decorated versions of the traditional pistols were produced – mostly in such cities as London and Birmingham.

Not only did Scotland produce pistols of unusual design; many of their early long guns were distinctively finished. Some were exotically made with stocks of Brazil wood and rather narrow, often gradually curved butts. Fluting and carving in the wood was commonly carried out, but trigger guards were very seldom fitted to these guns. By the 18th century, the characteristic Scottish features were disappearing from the weapons produced in Scotland and their appearance became very similar to English weapons of the same period. Firearm production in the Highlands was carried out in a number of places including Dundee, Stirling, Edinburgh and especially a small Perthshire village named Doune.

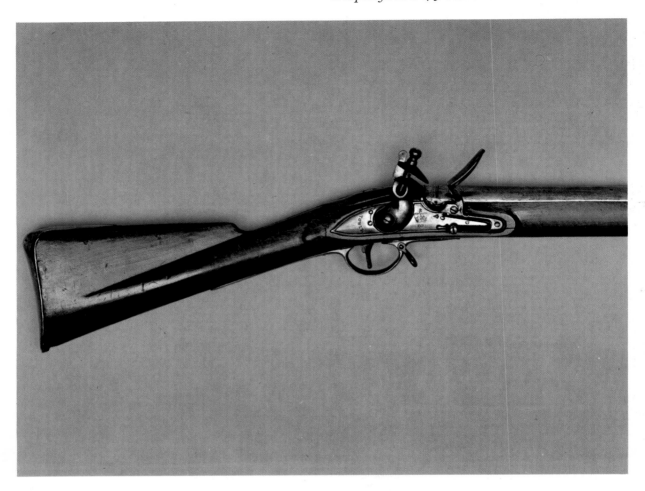

Military flintlocks

THE low cost of manufacturing match-locks encouraged governments of the 16th and 17th centuries to issue these arms to their troops, so the flintlock did not become general issue until the late 17th century. In Britain, supplies of military weapons were controlled by the Master of Ordnance who was responsible for ordering, quality and design. The weapons were manufactured by commercial makers and examined before acceptance and, consequently, most of the early military weapons bear the maker's name inscribed on the lockplate.

About 1710–20 the best known of all British military long arms was introduced, and later acquired the name of **Brown Bess.** The earliest version had a very long barrel, of 46 inches, and shortly afterwards a model with a shorter barrel, of 42 inches, was also introduced. The shorter weapon was adopted about 1768 and remained the standard weapon until 1794. At this date a new pattern was introduced, for the heavy demand of the Napoleonic wars necessitated the mass supply of muskets. The East India Company were

using a musket with a 39-inch barrel which was cheap and easily manufactured, so this became the official pattern. In 1802, production of a **New Land musket** was begun and this continued in use until the middle of the 19th century.

Developments in the style of military flintlock pistols were also mostly concerned with barrel length and minor changes in the furniture. Most early pistols had 12-inch barrels, but soon these were reduced to 10 inches and later to 8 inches. Some of the larger pistols designed for naval use had belt hooks–consequently, they became known as **Sea Service pistols.**

Most government weapons bear some official marking. On English weapons, the imprint was a crown and the royal cipher, ranging from "CR" for Carolus Rex (Charles) to "Victoria Regina". All military weapons also bore the date of manufacture, but this practice was abandoned in 1763, much to the regret of later collectors. In America, British weapons were, of course, standard until 1776 when the Revolutionary War broke out. The creation of United States arsenals naturally led to the introduction of a native-made product.

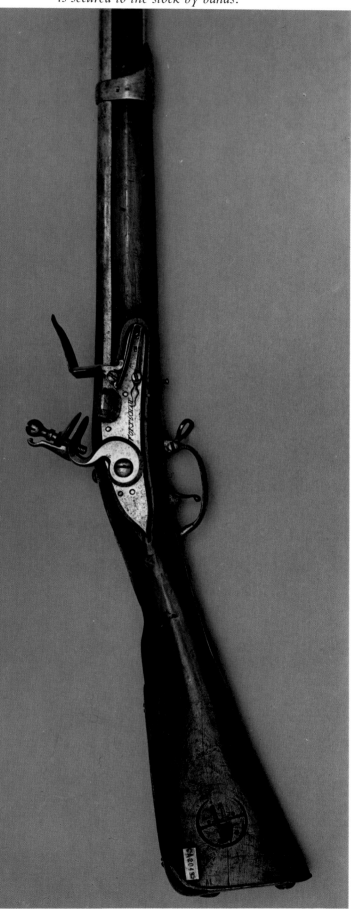

This 18th-century Bavarian infantry flintlock roughly equivalent to the British Brown Bess. It differs in having a reinforced breech and the barrel is secured to the stock by bands.

A private of the Royal North British Fusiliers, 1742.

The first musket, known as the **Springfield Flintlock Musket Model 1795,** was based on the French model of 1763 and bore on the lockplate an eagle with wings outstretched and the letters US. It had a black walnut stock and a barrel $44\frac{1}{2}$ inches long. Those made under contract usually carried the maker's name inscribed on the lockplate.

Pistols were not made at Springfield and a contract for military pistols was awarded to Simeon North of Berlin, Connecticut in March, 1799. These pistols fired a ball of .69 inches diameter and had an $8\frac{1}{2}$-inch barrel. Later pistols were made at the other US arsenal at Harpers Ferry.

On the continent of Europe a great variety of pistols and muskets were produced for the armies; most bear some identifying marks to indicate that they are government property. During the Napoleonic period it was the practice to award *fusils d'honneur* to soldiers who distinguished themselves. Many of the military weapons made at that time bear, in addition to government marks, a variety of letters and numbers indicating the unit or arsenal which held the weapon.

Rifling

ALL early firearms were inaccurate and the general standard of marksmanship extremely low. In battle this was not necessarily a great disadvantage, for firing was carried out mostly by volley. For hunters, scouts and skirmishers inaccuracy was a more serious handicap and efforts were made to overcome the problem.

Any number of factors could affect the flight of the bullet or send the missile off course. A major factor was the drag of the inside surface of the barrel on the bullet as it left the muzzle; the last point of contact could fractionally change the course of the bullet in almost any direction. Bullet shape and weight were also important factors. Since these could never be absolutely controlled, the solution was to neutralize them as far as possible. If the bullet could be made to spin in flight, then many of the variations would be largely canceled out: one way to produce this spin was to start the bullet rotating while it was still in the barrel. To do this, a series of shallow grooves were cut on the inside surface of the barrel. The bullet was made to engage with these grooves and follow them on its journey along the barrel and since they were in the form of a spiral, the bullet was made to spin. These grooves were known as **rifling** and a musket with this modification was known as a **rifle.**

Experiments in this field were begun quite early, but severe technical problems limited development.

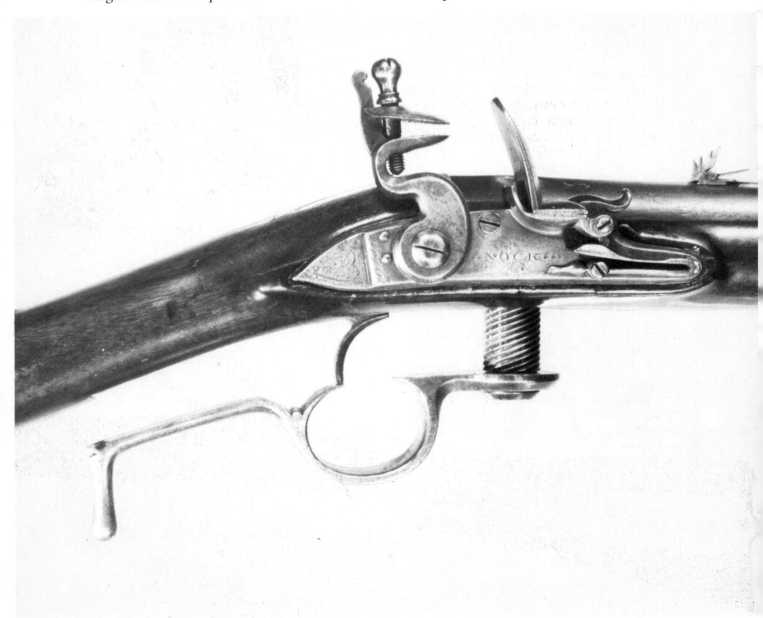

The Baker rifle

ALTHOUGH the principle of rifling was understood and various European units were issued with rifles during the 17th and 18th centuries, the British army had to wait until the 19th century to possess the rifle in quantity. In 1800 it was decided to hold a series of comparative tests to select a British rifle. The barrel chosen was one made by Ezekiel Baker, a London gunmaker: it had seven grooves which made a quarter turn in the length of the barrel so that the bullet was rotated through 90 degrees before it left the muzzle. The **Baker rifle** was well made with a solid wooden stock and a substantial barrel. The furniture was of brass and the trigger guard so shaped as to afford a good grip for the shooter. In the butt was a patch box, covered by a brass lid. In order to leave the sights clear, there was a stout bar at the side of the barrel, near the muzzle, and on to this was fixed the sword bayonet.

To make full use of the rifle, an experimental Rifle Corps was formed from detachments supplied from various regiments. The new body paraded for the first time on 1st April 1800 at Horsham in Surrey and was later known as the 95th Regiment. Since the new riflemen were intended to act mainly as skirmishers, they were dressed in green uniforms so that they might more easily merge into the background. The accuracy of these new weapons was so apparent that soon almost all the armies in Europe were, at least partially, equipped with rifles of one form or another.

Henry Beaufoys, writing in 1808, thought this was how the well-dressed and fully-equipped rifleman should look. On the ground can be seen the leather cover which fitted over the lock when the weapon was not in use.

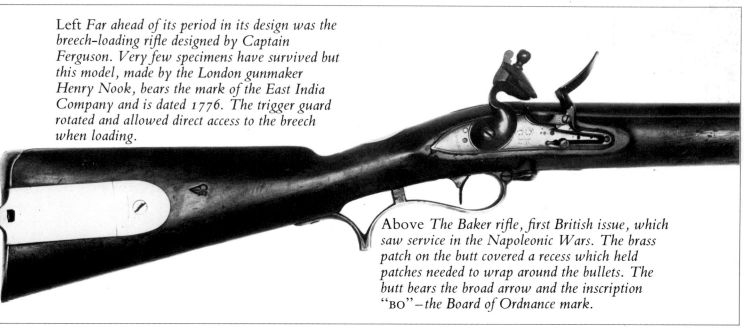

Left *Far ahead of its period in its design was the breech-loading rifle designed by Captain Ferguson. Very few specimens have survived but this model, made by the London gunmaker Henry Nook, bears the mark of the East India Company and is dated 1776. The trigger guard rotated and allowed direct access to the breech when loading.*

Above *The Baker rifle, first British issue, which saw service in the Napoleonic Wars. The brass patch on the butt covered a recess which held patches needed to wrap around the bullets. The butt bears the broad arrow and the inscription "BO"—the Board of Ordnance mark.*

Danish 1841 percussion pistol of unusual design— the hammer is fitted beneath the barrel. This pistol was patented in 1833 by N. Lobnitz.

Right Percussion, rifled carbine, officially adopted May 1856. It fired a .577-inch bullet and had five grooves.

The percussion cap

THE flintlock was simple, effective and generally reliable but it was not without its faults. Misfires were not uncommon and each piece of flint was reckoned to be reliable for thirty shots only. The priming was also a potential source of weakness, since wind or rain could dispose of it at the crucial moment of firing. Perhaps most annoying for the serious shooter was the hang-fire–the delay between pulling the trigger and the explosion. The hang-fire was small but appreciable, for it took time for the flint to scrape along the face of the frizzen, the sparks to fall into and fire the priming, and for the flash to pass through the touch hole and ignite the main charge. If the hunter did not make due allowance for this delay while aiming at a moving target, then a miss was certain. What was needed was a quicker and more reliable means of producing a flash to ignite the powder.

The solution was found by a Scottish clergyman, the Reverend Alexander Forsyth, who was a keen hunter as well as an amateur chemist. During his studies he had come across **fulminates** (a group of unstable chemicals which, when struck, "exploded" with a flash). The problem remained how best to deposit a small quantity of the fulminate in position. In 1807 Forsyth took out his patent for a "scent bottle" which deposited a few grains of fulminate into the touch hole where they were detonated by the blow of a hammer.

Forsyth's scent bottle proved a little too complex for general adoption, but he had very clearly pointed the way for future development. There were many attempts to overcome the limitations of his system: they included putting the fulminate into small tubes, between thin pieces of paper or in metal squares.

The system which proved most practical was the copper **percussion cap.** (It is not at all certain who invented the cap and many laid claim to the honor). The cap consisted of a small tube closed at one end, on which was deposited a thin coating of fulminate. The cap was placed over a small tube–the nipple– with a tiny hole drilled through it leading into the breech and so to the charge of powder. A solid nosed arm, the hammer, replaced the cock and flint and this struck the cap to force it against the nipple and so detonate the fulminate. To prevent accidents which could be caused by the cap splitting, the nose of the hammer was hollowed out so that the tip enclosed the cap and nipple. Caps were simple, safe and reliable and soon became the universal method of producing ignition. Another virtue of the new system was that flintlock weapons could easily be converted by the pillar method. Frizzen, spring and pan were removed and the cock was replaced by a hammer.

Percussion caps were used on very many types of weapons and opened the way for the modern cartridge arm. Armies were slow to adopt the new system and Britain only did so in 1839.

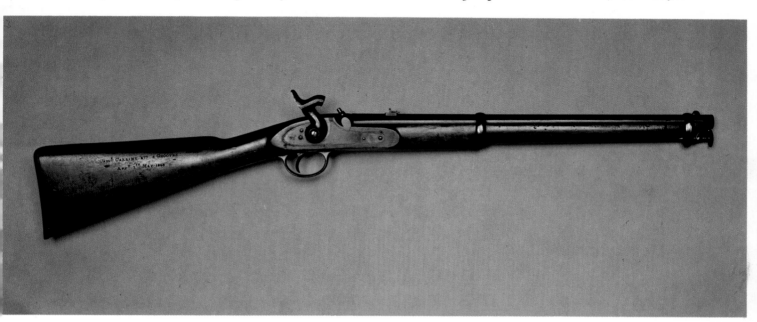

Bottom *A superb pair of percussion dueling pistols in case with all accessories, including small mallet, bullet mold, rods and powder flask. The* *items are set in a contoured case following the European fashion. The entire set was made by Bartolomaeus Joseph Kuchenreuter III, about 1850.*

Below *This is a rare sporting or target rifle by Isaac Rivière and uses his lock, which was patented in 1825. This resembles the boxlock used on many pocket pistols. The weapon has a fine pistol grip with grotesque butt cap and a very heavy, octagonal barrel.*

Opposite *A page from the Illustrated London News of November 8th, 1862, which illustrates some of the weapons from the 1862 International Exhibition. At the top are some sporting guns of the period; nos 11 and 12 are French and very ornate, whilst no. 13 is an English breech loading gun. No. 17 is a Swiss target rifle.*

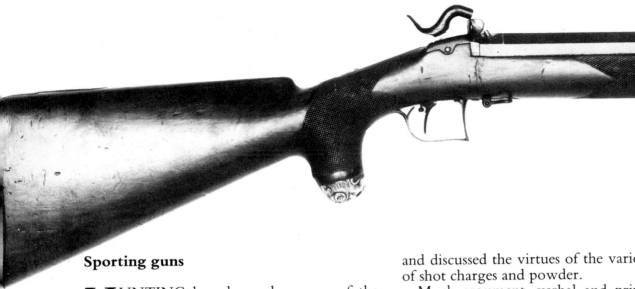

Sporting guns

HUNTING has always been one of the most popular occupations of the rich and leisured and in the 17th century shooting began to replace the older forms of the sport. At this time there appeared specialized guns with very long barrels for firing shot. These fowling pieces were based on the belief that a long barrel gave the powder a longer time to burn and therefore built up more power, giving greater range. Their great length made these weapons clumsy and most were used for shooting from fixed positions. Shorter, lighter guns were also made and their performance was improved by a number of inventions which speeded up ignition and permitted even shorter barrels. Since the barrel was shortened and therefore lighter, it became possible to make guns with two barrels and from the early 18th century these became increasingly popular. The adoption of the percussion cap increased their popularity. New styles of locks were produced: back action locks were commonly used on these sporting guns and had the main spring set behind the hammer. Stocks were usually simple but well-made and a few top-quality examples were sold in cases, sometimes with extra barrels.

A great deal of time was spent on the choice and care of a good gun and certain London gunmakers often acquired their reputations on the quality of their sporting guns. The **Manton brothers** in particular were highly regarded and of the two, Joseph was considered by most to be the superior.

Numerous books on hunting were written and discussed the virtues of the various forms of shot charges and powder.

Much argument, verbal and printed, was devoted to the question of which was the best type of gun but there was little dispute about one fact: the barrel was of prime importance in the construction of a first-class gun, needing care and much labor in its production. Trueness of aim and strength of metal were the maker's twin goals and tremendous care was taken to achieve them. Methods used by different makers varied slightly, but most used a sandwich of steel and iron strips – up to 12 layers. The strips were then welded solid and drawn into long square bars which were heated again and twisted like a rope; this gradually shortened the bar and made it round. These shorter bars were now welded, a little at a time, and gradually wound round a former. Most barrels were made in at least two sections, which were heated and welded together. On top-quality barrels the weld was so cleverly done as to be virtually invisible. The uniting of the layers of steel and iron and the twisting and bending all produced variations in the texture of the metal and when the barrel had been finished and browned these patterns were emphasized.

Since this method of construction was generally limited to very good-quality pieces, some manufacturers of low-price guns tried to produce the same effect by cheaper, simpler methods. Some sporting guns were made with two barrels, one of which was rifled, the other for normal shot. English sporting guns were normally fairly plain, but many European ones had stocks embellished by carving and, occasionally, inlay.

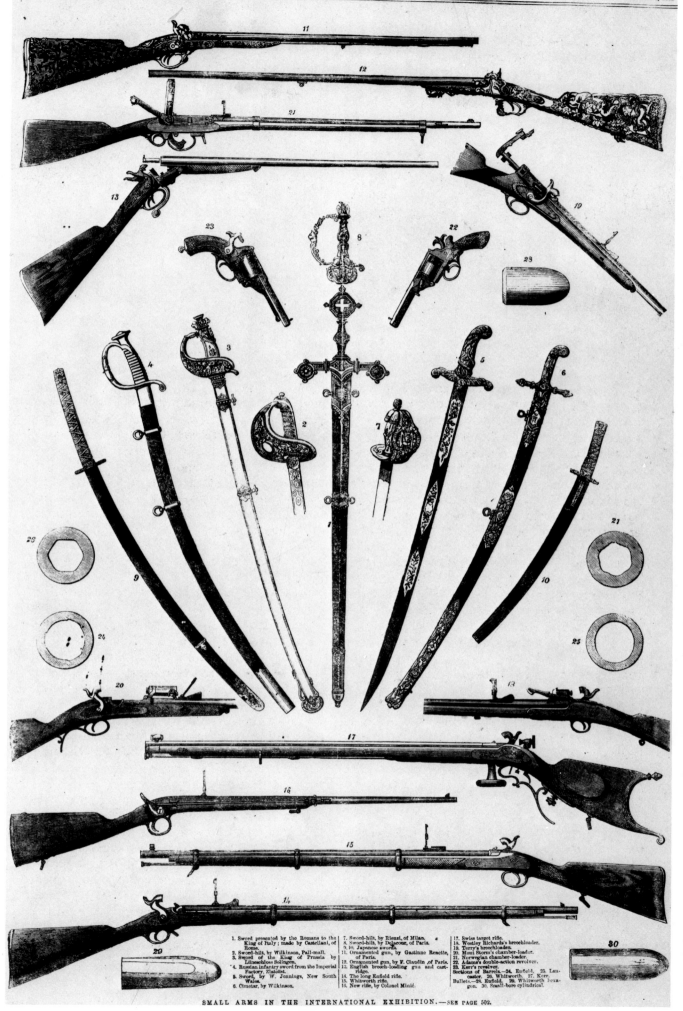

1. Sword presented by the Romans to the King of Italy; made by Castellani, of Rome.
2. Sword-hilt, by Wilkinson, Pall-mall.
3. Sword of the King of Prussia by Hoesschloss Salingen.
4. Russian infantry sword from the Imperial Factory, Zlatoüst.
5. Sword by W. Jennings, New South Wales.
6. Cimetar, by Wilkinson.

7. Sword-hilt, by Rienzi, of Milan.
8. Sword-hilt, by Delacour, of Paris.
9. 10. Japanese swords.
11. Ornamented gun, by Gastinne Renette, of Paris.
12. Ornamented gun, by F. Claudin, of Paris.
13. English breech-loading gun and cartridge.
14. The long Enfield rifle.
15. Whitworth rifle.
16. New rifle, by Colonel Minié.

17. Swiss target rifle.
18. Westley Richards's breechloader.
19. Terry's breechloader.
20. Mont Storm's chamber-loader.
21. Norwegian chamber-loader.
22. Adams's double-action revolver.
23. Kerr's revolver.
Sections of Barrels.—34. Enfield. 25. Lancaster. 26. Whitworth. 27. Kerr.
Bullets.—28. Enfield. 29. Whitworth hexagon. 30. Small-bore cylindrical.

SMALL ARMS IN THE INTERNATIONAL EXHIBITION.—SEE PAGE 502.

The Brunswick rifle

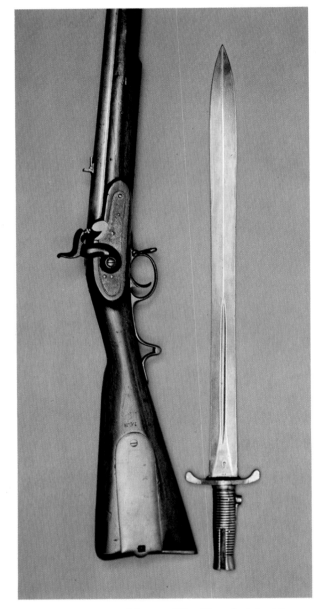

THE Baker flintlock rifle was a serviceable and effective weapon, but it was not without its faults and eventually it became necessary to replace it. Several European weapons were studied, tested and rejected in Britain for various reasons. Eventually George Lovell, the man charged to select a replacement, tested a rifle developed in the German State of Brunswick and selected this for use by the British army.

Superficially, the **Brunswick rifle** resembled the Baker in appearance being the same size, although a little heavier, with a long, heavy, wooden stock and a shaped trigger guard. The butt housed a compartment for patches and tools, covered with a brass lid held in place by a spring clip. There was a bayonet bar by the side of the muzzle as on the Baker. A back action percussion lock was fitted on the earlier models, but later ones had a conventional lock.

It was the barrel of this gun that was distinctive. Most rifling consisted of a series of grooves, usually five or more, but the Brunswick rifle used only two, which completed one full turn in the length of the 39½-inch barrel. The bullet was cast with a narrow, raised belt around its circumference and had to be loaded into the barrel so that the belt engaged with the two grooves. It was an accurate weapon and could fire 10 shots in just over 7 minutes, a satisfactory rate for a muzzle loading rifle. The Brunswick was first made in 1837 and was replaced in the early 1850s.

Above The Brunswick rifle acquired an unhappy reputation and was certainly rather heavy. It used a bullet with a raised band around it. In many ways it resembled the Baker rifle including a bar, fitted by the side of the muzzle, which was used to hold the brass-hilted bayonet.

Right Jacob double-barreled rifle fitted with back action locks. The stock extends only half-way along the barrel and there is a patch box set into the butt.

Muzzle of a Brunswick rifle with the tops of the twin grooves into which the belted bullet slipped. The end of the heavy ramrod can be seen as well as the boss which took the bayonet.

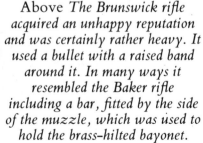

Jacob's rifle

THE Brunswick rifle was in service with the British Army for some fourteen years and was revived for a period when it was supplied to the Government of East India. It was the object of much criticism, but it must have had some virtues, for Lovell, its patron, was an astute man.

The Brunswick did not satisfy one man, John Jacob, a major in the Scinde Irregular Horse. He tested it over a period and sought to improve on it by introducing a ball with two belts, crossing at right angles, for a barrel with four grooves. He offered this modified rifle to the East India Company but they rejected it. Jacob was not discouraged and pursued his idea: he kept the four-groove rifling, but used a large, cylindro-conical bullet with four projecting lugs which engaged with the grooves. He was ahead of his time in fitting these massive bullets with **explosive heads.**

In 1856, he produced a new version which had two barrels side-by-side, each with its deep, four-groove rifling. Although **Jacob's rifle** had only a half stock it was very heavy, a factor made even more pronounced by the longest bayonet ever used in the British army – 2 feet 6 inches long. Jacob made his rifles with four sharp projections on the inside of the barrel, near the breech. These were intended to rip open the paper case of a cartridge rammed down the barrel. In 1888, he created the 1st Regiment of Jacob's Rifles, which later became the 30th Regiment of Bombay Native Infantry.

The Colt

IF one man's name has become synonymous with firearms, then it must be that of **Samuel Colt**; for many people, every revolver is a Colt. He was born near Hartford, Connecticut in July 1814, and even as a boy showed signs of the flair for inventiveness and publicity that was to mark his life in years to come.

Samuel made a voyage to the east on board the brig Corvo in 1830. It was during this voyage to India and back that he conceived the idea for a really practical working **revolver**, something which had eluded gunmakers for centuries. Basically the idea was very simple and consisted of one arm which pushed round the cylinder and another which locked it in position for firing. The entire sequence of events was motivated by the simple action of cocking the hammer.

Colt carved a working model of his idea in wood and took out a patent in London in December, 1835 and in America in February, 1836. A company was formed and started production of a five-shot revolver known as the **Paterson model**. Despite its obvious virtues, the weapon did not attract orders and the company failed. Colt was not the sort of man to give in easily and in 1847 was once more manufacturing a heavy revolver weighing over four pounds and firing a bullet .44 inches in diameter. This revolver was produced primarily for the military market, but it marked the turning point in Colt's career; from then on he never looked back.

Having broken into the market, Colt was

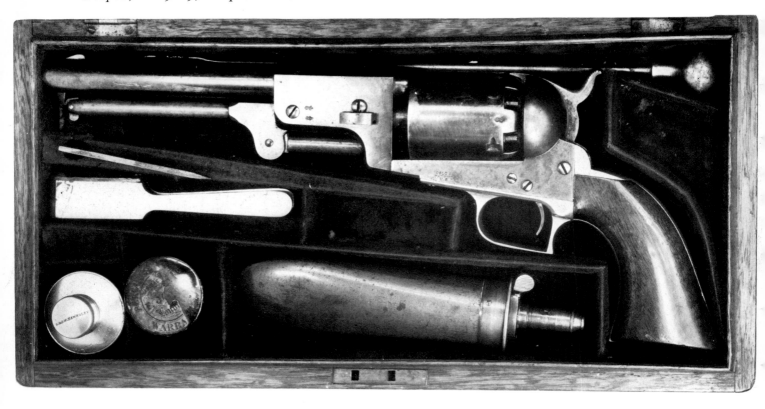

able to expand his range of products, catering more for the civilian market. He produced a much smaller revolver (the **pocket** model) firing a bullet .31 inches in diameter, then a larger revolver (the **belt** or **Navy** model) firing a .36-inch bullet. Large numbers of these weapons were produced, for Colt was able to use modern, almost "production line" methods.

The cylinder of a Colt revolver was engraved with various scenes of action. The early heavier models had an indian fight, the pocket version a stage coach hold-up and the Navy model a battle at sea. Samuel Colt seldom missed an opportunity of getting his products mentioned and his advertisements were to be seen everywhere. He exhibited at the Great Exhibition held in London in 1851 and gave special presentation revolvers to people he felt might be impressed and, even more important, might be of use to him in the future. Encouraged by the response in England and feeling that there was a very good potential market, he set up a factory in London. Only pocket and Navy revolvers were manufactured in this London factory; he imported other models and sold them through a shop in Pall Mall, London. In this venture, however, Colt had misjudged his market: demand did not justify his hopes and the factory closed in 1857.

In 1857, Colt changed the design of one of his revolvers and introduced a model known as the **New Model Pocket** or the **Roots Side Hammer.** This had the hammer mounted outside the frame—a very different design from all Colt's other percussion revolvers.

His revolvers consisted of three main parts: a barrel, a cylinder and a frame. The cylinder slipped over a rod fitted to the frame and the barrel was fitted to the frame by engaging with the rod and the base of the frame. The barrel was held in position by a wedge which passed through the lug below the barrel and through the rod of the frame, so locking the two parts firmly together. This type of construction was known as an open frame; the Roots model differed in that the barrel was permanently fixed to the frame which had a top bar above the cylinder.

The method of loading and firing a Colt revolver was simple: first the hammer was drawn back to the first position, at which point a click was heard; this was the half cock, and the cylinder was now free to rotate. Powder was poured into each chamber and a bullet placed in the mouth was then pressed home by operating the articulated ramrod beneath the barrel. The routine was repeated for each of the six chambers. Copper percussion caps were placed on the nipples, the hammer was released and carefully lowered and the weapon was ready. To fire a shot, the hammer was drawn right back and the

Close-up view of the cylinder and hammer of Colt's revolving rifle; the nipples which receive the cap can be clearly seen.

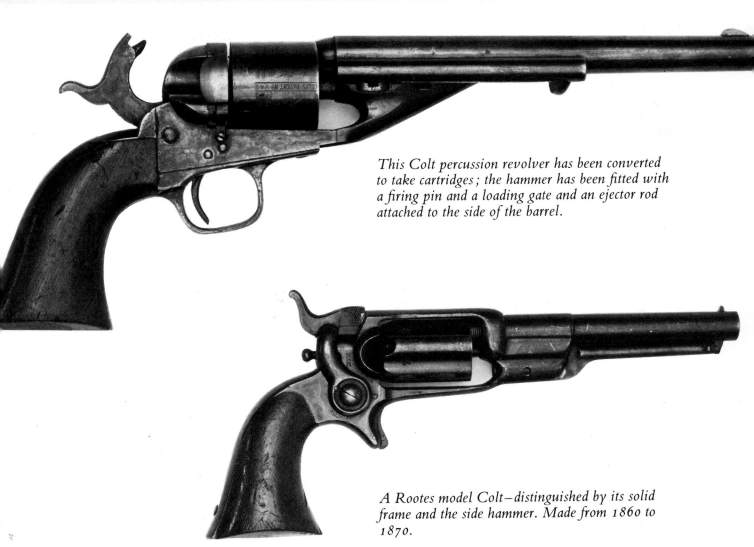

This Colt percussion revolver has been converted to take cartridges; the hammer has been fitted with a firing pin and a loading gate and an ejector rod attached to the side of the barrel.

A Rootes model Colt—distinguished by its solid frame and the side hammer. Made from 1860 to 1870.

51

trigger pressed, allowing it to fall forward and strike the cap.

Although Colt was known primarily for his revolvers, he also experimented with long arms – which were basically his revolver cylinder and action fitted with a shoulder stock and a long barrel. In 1861 he was given the rank of colonel in the 1st Regiment of Colt Revolving Rifles. He held the rank for but a short time, from 16th May to 20th June, for he had a disagreement with the Governor of Connecticut who, as a result, promptly canceled the grant.

Colt died at his home, Armsmear, in January 1862, aged 48, but his name had, by then, become established. Today copies of his early percussion revolvers are still being made and the factory which he founded still produces firearms. Colt was a flamboyant character, but his revolver design was reliable and his production methods efficient. A certain number of revolvers were specially decorated and engraved and these were made either to special order or as presentation pieces for a celebrity or friend. Most of the models were sold in a wooden case complete with all accessories including bullet mold, powder flask and a container of caps.

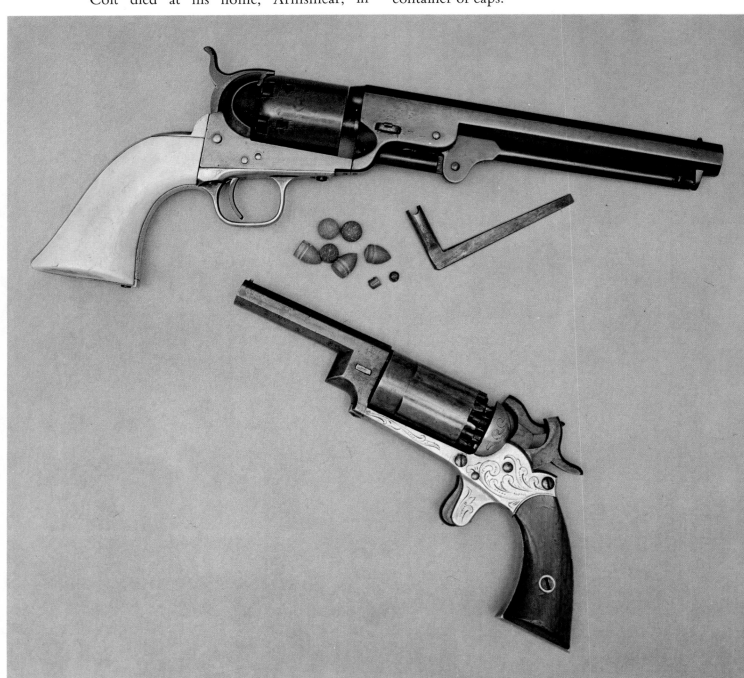

Opposite top *Fine Colt navy revolver with ivory grips and a brass trigger guard. This was one of Colt's most popular models and was in production from 1851 to about 1873.*
Below is the L-shaped key for unscrewing the nipples, together with caps and bullets, round and conical.

Bottom *The Walch revolver of 1859, which used a cylinder holding 2 loads in each chamber. The two hammers were operated by a single trigger; one hammer fired the front charge and the second the rear charge.*

Below *A Tranter, percussion revolver with its case, complete with all accessories such as mold, powder flask and tins of caps, grease and bullets. This model does not have the double trigger found on the earlier revolvers by this maker.*

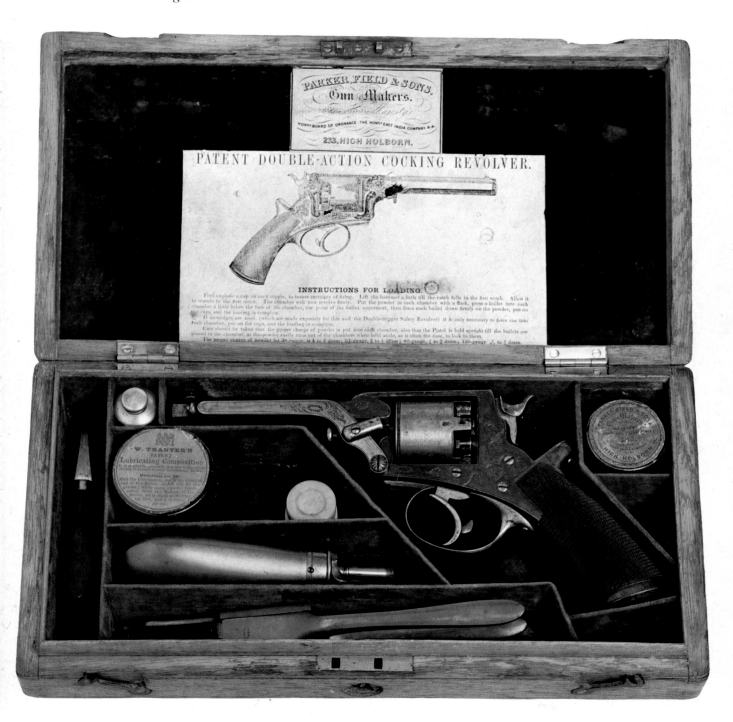

The Adams

WHEN Colt exhibited his revolvers at the Great Exhibition of 1851, there was no real British competitor in this field apart from Robert Adams. In 1851, Adams had obtained a patent for a percussion revolver, but whether it was available in quantity in that year is doubtful. The **Adams revolver** differed from Colt's production in manufacture, construction and design. It was a five-shot weapon (Colt's was six-shot) and it had a solid frame fashioned in one piece with the barrel. The bullets were loaded without the aid of a ramrod and were of a special design with a spiked tail which pierced a wad. It was in the action that there was the main difference, for Adam's revolver was self-cocking. On a Colt revolver, the hammer had a spur which was engaged with the thumb and pulled back to rotate the cylinder and cock the mechanism; pressure on the trigger released the hammer. On an Adam's revolver there was no spur on the hammer: the cylinder was rotated, the mechanism cocked and the weapon fired all by direct pressure on the trigger.

In 1855 the revolver was altered to incorporate the action designed by a Lt Frederick Beaumont. This new **Beaumont-Adams revolver** offered the best of both worlds, for it could be cocked by pulling back the hammer with the thumb or simply by pressing the trigger. There was much contemporary controversy about the comparative virtues and faults of the Adams and Colt revolvers, but both had failings and advantages and there was probably little to choose between them.

The Tranter

ALTHOUGH many British gunmakers flourished during the 19th century, a few names stand out, among them that of **William Tranter**. He was a very successful Birmingham gunmaker producing a great variety of weapons but he is probably best known for his unusual **double trigger, percussion revolvers**. These were made using an Adams frame and barrel but with a long trigger, the lower part of which protruded through the bottom of the trigger guard. Pressure on the trigger by the middle finger of the hand holding the butt caused the cylinder to rotate and cocked the mechanism, but it did not fire the shot. To fire, the second, smaller trigger, which was built into the longer one and housed within the trigger guard, had to be pressed. This system offered the advantages of single action without the need to relax the grip when pulling back the hammer with the thumb, and it also permitted a more rapid rate of fire. The revolver was produced in a variety of sizes and with minor differences of detail, but in 1856 Tranter patented and later began producing a revolver with a completely different mechanism. In general appearance it closely resembled a Beaumont-Adams revolver except for the small, square block set on the back of the trigger which pressed on and released the sear to fire the weapon.

Another well-known name of the period was that of the **Webley brothers**, who produced a variety of percussion revolvers from the late 1850s onwards.

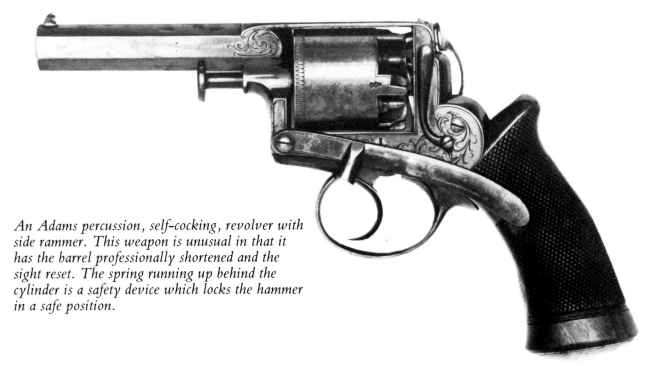

An Adams percussion, self-cocking, revolver with side rammer. This weapon is unusual in that it has the barrel professionally shortened and the sight reset. The spring running up behind the cylinder is a safety device which locks the hammer in a safe position.

Engraving showing the inventor, Robert Adams,
loading one of his revolvers which he had
presented to HRH Prince Albert.

E.EVANS.Sc

Robt Adams

A breech-loading flintlock rifle made by John Hall of Maine, USA. He used a breech block which tipped up to allow it to be charged with powder and ball. The block was then pushed down and held in place by a spring latch. It dates from about 1820.

Breech-loading weapons

EARLY cannon were loaded with powder and ball not at the muzzle but at the breech; this was very difficult to do on smaller firearms. To load at the breech, there had to be an opening to permit the insertion of powder and ball. Before the explosion took place, the opening obviously had to be closed and securely locked shut. It was the solution to this problem that eluded designers for centuries, since most breech-loading weapons allowed far too much gas to escape, so reducing the power of the bullet as well as constituting a danger to the shooter.

The first really important new idea was produced by Isaac de la Chaumette in 1704. He proposed that the barrel should have a screwed plug attached at the lower end to the trigger guard. One turn of the trigger guard lowered the plug so that powder and ball could be placed directly into the breech. The trigger guard was then turned in the opposite direction, the plug replaced and the weapon was ready. After various modifications this system was used by Captain Patrick Ferguson in his breech-loading rifle of 1776. He very clearly demonstrated its efficiency, but the British army was not really interested and the idea was not developed. Later, in America, the **Sharps rifle** of 1848 used the trigger guard to lower a block which gave access to the breech for a cartridge. The rifle had to be cocked by hand and the priming was dispensed in the form of small pellets.

Cartridges

LOOSE powder was always a hazard to the shooter and at an early date the powder flask was introduced. While it was safer and more convenient, it was, nonetheless, a hindrance because, by some means or other, the powder had to be measured. Musketeers overcame this problem by using a bandolier whose suspended containers each held a pre-measured charge of powder. An even more convenient system was the use of a disposable container, a cartridge. In the 16th century they were of stout paper rolled into a tube and filled with powder, topped with a bullet and then tied at the top. When loading, the cartridge was torn or bitten, a pinch of the enclosed powder placed in the pan for priming and the rest poured down the barrel followed by the paper and ball. This design was retained throughout the 17th, 18th and first half of the 19th centuries but it was of limited use and most unsatisfactory for use in any breech-loading weapon.

The earliest form of modern metallic cartridge can be said to have been designed by a Swiss, Johannes Pauly, in 1812, but the idea was not really developed until 1854 when **Smith and Wesson**, an American firm of gunmakers, patented a copper-cased cartridge with a small charge of priming fitted at the center of the base. In 1860 this same firm patented the rimfire cartridge in which the priming was deposited on the inside of the outer edge of the base of the cartridge. The hammer of the weapon struck on the rim to detonate the priming–fulminate–which in turn fired the powder enclosed within the case. However, the type which was to become standard had the priming set in the center of the base.

Bullets

With the gradually expanding use of rifling and the development of breech-loading weapons, there were many new ideas about bullets. With smooth bore, muzzle-loading weapons, a round bullet, which was not too tight, was quite adequate, but for a rifle the bullet had to fit snugly. If, however, the fit was too tight, then the rifle was extremely difficult to load, although the use of a greasy piece of material wrapped around the bullet did help. In the 19th century there were many experiments to discover the best shape of bullet.

The first really simple, practical solution was that devised by an inventor named Minie who proposed a fairly loose-fitting bullet with a wooden plug in the base. When the powder was burned, the expanding gas forced the plug into the bullet, spreading it slightly so that the sides firmly gripped the rifling. It was soon realized that the same result could be obtained without the wooden plug, which was then abandoned. During the 19th century the bullet diameter gradually decreased. Brown Bess and other 18th and early 19th century military weapons used bullets of about .75-inch diameter, but by the mid-century this was down to .577 inch and later still down to .303 or less. By the 19th century, machines had been devised to press bullets out of lead "wire" and the older method of melting lead and casting them was largely abandoned. Many bullets were also coated with thin layers of harder metals to prevent them being melted by the excessive heat of the newly discovered propellents.

Left to right
.36 bullet for Navy Colt model 1851.
.45 wadded bullet for Adams self-cocking revolver.
.45 bullet for Adams revolver.
.577-inch Ball for an Enfield rifle.
.75-inch Ball for a Brown Bess musket.
.577 Enfield rifle bullet.
Hollow nose 4 belt bullet for Jacob's Rifle.
Sako .38 special.
Martini–Henry rifle.
Kynock 360 Nitro Express.
Holland & Holland Magnum express for big game.

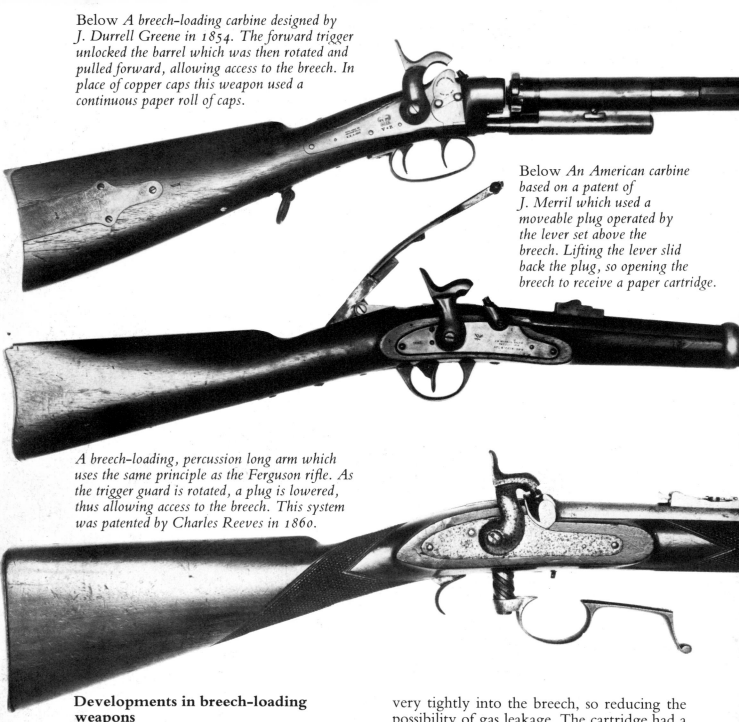

Below *A breech-loading carbine designed by J. Durrell Greene in 1854. The forward trigger unlocked the barrel which was then rotated and pulled forward, allowing access to the breech. In place of copper caps this weapon used a continuous paper roll of caps.*

Below *An American carbine based on a patent of J. Merril which used a moveable plug operated by the lever set above the breech. Lifting the lever slid back the plug, so opening the breech to receive a paper cartridge.*

A breech-loading, percussion long arm which uses the same principle as the Ferguson rifle. As the trigger guard is rotated, a plug is lowered, thus allowing access to the breech. This system was patented by Charles Reeves in 1860.

Developments in breech-loading weapons

THE development of metal-cased cartridges with built-in primers made possible the development of many new and more efficient firearms. In Britain, Colonel Boxer's cartridge was designed for the **Snider rifle** which had been adopted in 1864. The Snider action was chosen as the simplest and most economic method of converting the large stock of muzzle-loading weapons held by the government into breech loaders. Fitted at the breech was a metal block containing a pin which took the blow of the hammer and transferred it to the percussion cap set in the base of the cartridge. **Boxer's cartridge** had a brass case which, during the explosion, expanded to fit

very tightly into the breech, so reducing the possibility of gas leakage. The cartridge had a rim which seated against the end of the breech and the primer was set in the center of the base. In 1885 the case was improved, for the earlier form had tended to split.

Smokeless powder, a more efficient form of explosive, was increasingly adopted during the last decades of the 19th century and the first cartridges fitted with the new propellent were introduced around the 1890s. The new powder was not without some drawbacks, such as melting the bullet, but by the 1920s bullets were being jacketed to overcome this. Most cartridge cases could be reloaded by removing the old, fired primer and inserting a new one, refilling with powder and fitting in a fresh bullet.

The attack on the Magdala—an incident during the Abyssinian War on 13th April, 1868. The troops were armed mainly with Snider-Enfield rifles using a black powder cartridge—hence the great clouds of smoke.

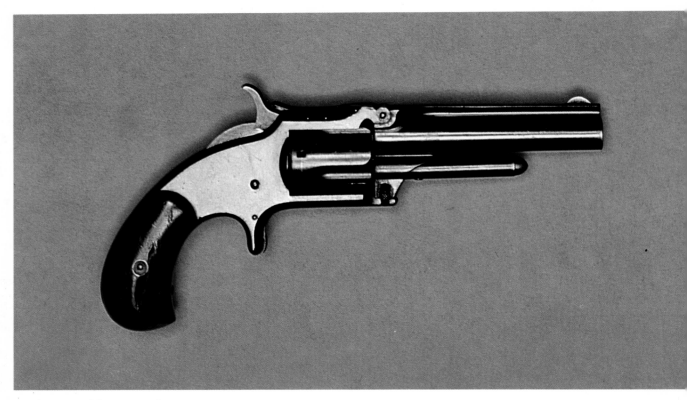

Early cartridge revolvers

SAMUEL Colt was well placed to reap the maximum benefit from the American firearms market: he held a master patent for systems in which cocking the hammer rotated the cylinder of a revolver. However, in 1857 his patent expired–an opportunity awaited by other gunmakers. Daniel Wesson and Horace Smith were planning to issue a revolver with a mechanically rotated cylinder but with improvements. They had acquired rights in a patent held by Rollin White, who had conceived the idea of drilling a chamber right through the cylinder and loading from the rear. Smith and Wesson were already hard at work developing a practical rimfire cartridge and they saw the immense possibilities of combining the two ideas. From 1857–1869 they held a monopoly of **breech-loading revolvers** in America. Their first issue fired a .22-inch diameter bullet and since the cartridge was small, they managed to fit seven shots around the cylinder. To unload, the barrel was tipped up, the cylinder removed and the empty cases pushed out by means of a metal rod situated below the barrel. In 1860, the firm issued their second model, essentially of the same design, which fired a .32-inch bullet. They made another very important innovation in 1869 when they produced a self-ejecting revolver. When the barrel was tipped forward and down, a small arm was pushed out from the center of the cylinder, so dislodging all the empty cases at once.

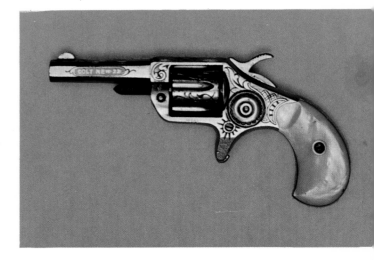

Top *A Smith and Wesson, breech-loading, .36 revolver with tip-up barrel for loading and bar beneath the barrel for the ejection of cases.*

Above *A Colt New Line .22-inch revolver, 2nd model. Fitted with mother-of-pearl grips and the body nickel plated. These seven-shot weapons were in production from 1876–77.*

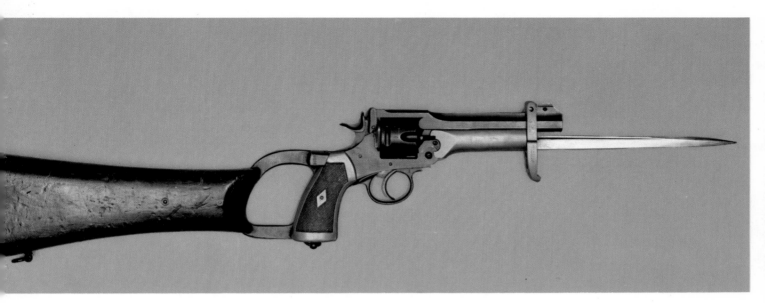

Early breech-loading revolvers

BRITISH makers were naturally concerned with the latest developments in the American market. They were also more fortunate, for the restrictions imposed in America by the Rollin White patent did not apply to them. They sought ways to convert existing weapons to take the new cartridges and a number of models were produced which could take different cylinders for rimfire or percussion use. In 1866 a metal cartridge, suitable for use in a revolver, was developed and John Adams, the brother of Robert, developed a **double action revolver** which would fire the metal .45-inch cartridge. The empty cases were ejected by a push rod mounted below the barrel; each case had to be cleared individually. The cartridges were loaded after swinging clear a metal plate, the gate, at the rear of the cylinder. In 1868, this revolver was officially adopted by the British army. Other British makers were soon in the market and cartridge revolvers were produced by the famous firms of Tranter and Webley. The introduction of cartridges made possible the manufacture of a whole host of small weapons intended for self-protection, re-placing the pocket pistol of the 18th century. Some of these curious weapons combined blades, knuckle dusters and revolvers while others were made flat and small to fit into the palm of the hand. With the development of the metal cartridge, the modern firearm had finally arrived and later changes were to be mostly of design and detail.

Above *British army Enfield revolver adopted in 1880, which fired a .476-inch bullet. It was a six-shot weapon with a rather unusual ejection system for the empty cases whereby the cylinder moved forward, leaving the cases which were then shaken out. This is the Mark I model.*

Top *The famous Colt Single Action Army revolver, introduced in 1873 and still a classic shooting weapon. It is simple in operation, rugged in construction and reliable. This model has been chambered for almost every caliber and made with a great range of barrel lengths. It was given a variety of names, including the Frontier and Peacemaker.*

Bottom *A departure from the usual run of Colt's weapons was this version of the Frontier revolver, for it was a double action model and the hammer could be cocked with the thumb or by pressing the trigger.*

Colt and cartridges

UNTIL 1857, Colt had flourished with no serious rivals, but after the expiry of his master patent he faced stiffer competition. Matters were made even more complicated by the fact that Smith and Wesson were not only producing revolvers but also using metal cartridges which could be loaded from the breech. Colt sought ways to beat his rivals' monopoly by using a metal cartridge which was not loaded at the breech. He chose a system invented by F. Alexander Thuer which required only a special cylinder so that the revolver could still be used with an ordinary percussion system, if desired. Thuer's cartridges were loaded from the front and the cases were ejected by dropping the hammer on a stud set in a ring fitted at the rear of the

special cylinder. It was apparently not a very successful system. However, in 1873, 11 years after Colt's death, the Colt concern introduced their most famous, center fire cartridge revolver, the **Single Action Army** model. It was loaded from the rear and the empty case was manually ejected by a push rod fitted below the barrel. It has been made to fire cartridges ranging from .22 inches up to .476 inches and with barrel lengths from 2 inches to 16 inches. This revolver was favored by many of the famous figures of the old wild West, for example Buffalo Bill and sheriff Bat Masterson. It has continued in production with only one break since 1873, and is still made today. In 1877, Colts produced a double action revolver (all previous models had been single action and required manual cocking).

Remington firearms

ANOTHER name well known in the field of American firearms was that of Remington. The family connection with guns began with Eliphalet Remington, in the early 19th century, and the business gradually expanded until by the middle of the century it was producing large quantities of arms. In 1859, the firm issued its first revolver which became very popular during the Civil War (1861–1865). Like Colts, the firm had some difficulty when Smith and Wesson began producing cartridge weapons, but they survived and went on to make many cartridge weapons. They specialized in small pocket weapons named after **Henry Deringer**. These were usually single-shot weapons although models with two and four barrels were made. The popularity of these weapons ensured a long production life for some models, stretching from 1866 to 1935. The first cartridge model produced by Remington was a small Derringer firing six shots. However, the most important contribution to firearm design made by Remingtons was probably their **rolling block** which was a very simple method of allowing breech loading. They manufactured a number of single-shot pistols, but in 1873 they introduced the first of their **New Line Revolvers** with five shots. In 1875 came their **Army Revolver**. One feature found on many Remington and other revolvers is the **sheath trigger**. This dispenses with a trigger guard and has the trigger set between two fixed plates with only a very small portion exposed to the risk of a knock and accidental discharge.

Top *Remington Army revolver of 1874, very similar in appearance to the Colt Single Action revolver. It fired a .44 bullet and was in production until 1889.*

Bottom *A Remington-Elliott derringer with four barrels. Each of the .32 rimfire cartridges was struck by a hammer which rotated as the ring trigger was operated. 1863–1888.*

Right *Borchardt self-loading pistol fitted with the shoulder stock, to which is attached the leather holster. The butt is well forward in order to accommodate the coiled spring which operated the mechanism.*

Right *Borchardt self-loading pistol fitted with the shoulder stock, to which is attached the leather holster. The butt is well forward in order to accommodate the coiled spring which operated the mechanism.*

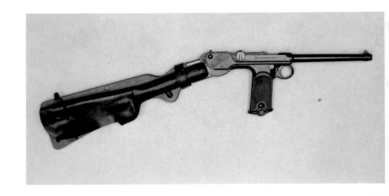

Below *Artillery Model Luger with $7\frac{1}{2}$ inch barrel fitted with holster, shoulder stock and snail magazine. These weapons were first issued in 1917. The model has an adjustable rear sight.*

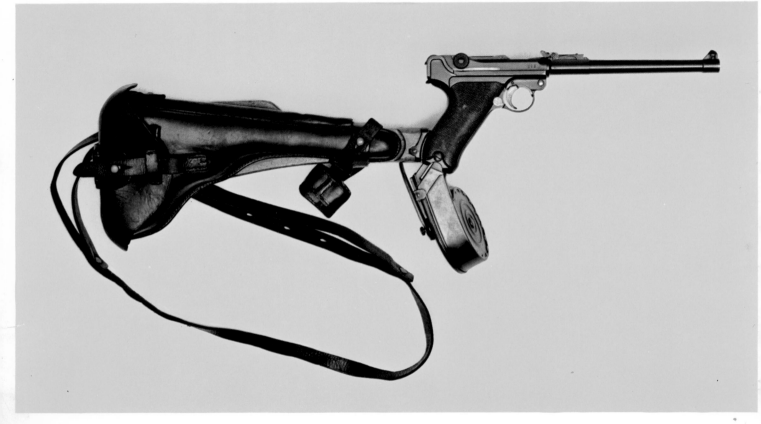

Automatic or self-loading pistols

A basic law of physics is that every action has an equal and opposite reaction; therefore, when a bullet left the barrel of a firearm there was always a kick in the opposite direction–known as the recoil. For centuries this phenomenon proved no more than a nuisance. However, towards the end of the 19th century many firearms designers became interested in utilizing this backward movement to eject the spent cartridge case, load a fresh one into the breech and cock the mechanism ready to fire another shot. In order to achieve this, there had to be a moving part: this could take many forms and the motive power could be generated either by the recoil or by using some of the gas created by the

explosion. The first **self-loading pistol** was made in 1893 to a patent granted to Hugo Borchardt in that year. Ejection and reloading of the pistol were achieved by a bolt which was attached to a jointed toggle arm. The design itself was sound, but the pistol was a little cumbersome in use and it fell to George Luger to modify the design and produce a self-loading pistol good enough for its manufacture to continue, virtually unchanged, until 1942. The pistol normally took a magazine holding eight rounds of 9-mm cartridges, although some magazines taking 32 rounds were made. A variety of barrel lengths were available, ranging from $3\frac{5}{8}$ inches up to 24 inches, but most had 4-inch barrels; the Naval model had one $5\frac{1}{2}$ inches long and the Artillery model a $7\frac{1}{2}$-inch barrel.

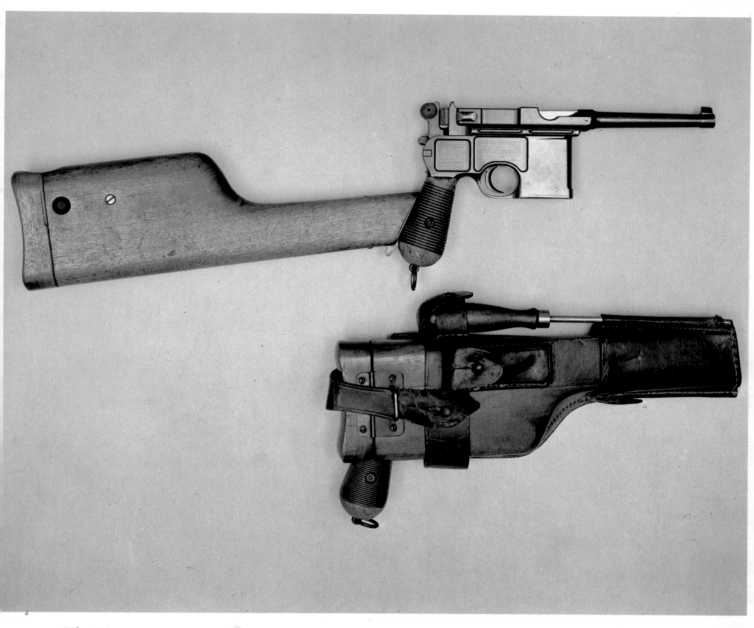

Mauser self-loading pistols with combined wooden holster and stock. The lower pistol has the carrying harness attached complete with the cleaning rod and compartment for spare magazine spring.

The Mauser

ANOTHER of the earliest of self-loading pistols was made by Peter Mauser, a manufacturer of rifles and cannon. His bolt-action rifle was to see service in the German army and he produced a number of revolvers. The **Mauser self-loader** was of unusual design, for the magazine was situated in front of the trigger and not contained inside the butt as on the Luger and other weapons. The first models were manufactured in 1896 and held ten rounds of .30 cartridges which were fed into the magazine from a clip, which was then removed. To start the action, a slide was pulled back and as each shot was fired, this slide moved forward and back again. The cartridge, like others for use in self-loading

pistols, had no rim but only a groove cut near the base. This arrangement was necessary, since a rim would prevent the cartridges sliding easily from the magazine into the breech. Fitted to the bolt on most self-loaders was a spring-operated claw which engaged with this groove and withdrew the case just before ejection. Mauser pistols of this type were usually supplied in a wooden holster which could be clipped on to the butt, thus converting the weapon into a carbine. Mauser automatics were popular in the East and many were supplied to the Chinese market as well as to Russia during the Revolutionary wars. In the 1930s, a special type known as **Schnell-Feuer-Pistole** was made: this model was, in effect, a sub-machine gun for it gave fully automatic fire.

Machine guns

IN a self-loading system the block, or slide, which moves backwards and forwards, is stopped after each cycle and stays locked until the trigger is pressed again. It makes no difference if the trigger is kept depressed, for the internal locking mechanism is designed to operate even in this condition. If, however, the mechanism is modified, the weapon will continue to fire until either the ammunition runs out or the trigger is released this is the principle of the true, automatic weapon or machine gun. Such weapons were not new

and as long ago as 1718 there was a hand-operated repeating gun. In 1862, Dr Richard Gatling demonstrated his gun which was hand operated and could maintain a high rate of fire. These and other similar weapons were of limited capability and it was not until 1884 that the first real machine gun was patented by Sir Hiram Maxim. He was of French stock, but was born in America and later became an English citizen. His gun was efficient and was adopted by several armies, including the British and German; the British used a modified form known as the **Vickers.** In the **Maxim** gun, cartridges were fed in on a

canvas belt holding 250 rounds, and so great was the heat generated during firing that the barrel was cooled by a water jacket. The Maxim or Vickers was fitted to a variety of tripods and stands and saw service fitted to aircraft in World War I. In 1895, John Browning developed a machine gun which used, not the recoil, but gas generated by the explosion to operate the mechanism.

It was during World War I that machine guns were first put to the practical test of war on a vast scale and soon they had virtually destroyed the cavalry and introduced a whole new concept of war. German and British mowed each other down with Maxims and Vickers while the French did their share with the **Hotchkiss**. This weapon was developed in the 1890s and used gas as the motive force, as did the Browning version, but the Hotchkiss method was far more efficient. It first saw service during the Russo-Japanese War of 1904–5 and was adopted by the French and continued to be their main machine gun until 1940. Cartridge feed was not by fabric belt but by means of metal strips of various lengths holding 30 or more catridges. Maxims, Brownings, Vickers and Hotchkiss were very substantial weapons and are usually classed as heavy machine guns. Lighter weapons for less static use were developed and among the most versatile and widely used was the **Lewis gun.** It was developed in 1910/11 by Lt Col. Isaac Lewis in America, but it was also manufactured in Belgium and Britain and was widely used by the British forces on sea, land and in the air. It was unusual in that it was fitted with a circular magazine. The Lewis gun saw service in many armies, but although the mechanism was the same, it was modified to fire different-sized ammunition.

Top *Cut-away detail of breech and bolt of the Lewis light machine gun with a circular magazine drum in position. The return spring can be seen and this is put under tension as gas from the exploding cartridges pushes back the bolt.*

Left *The Vickers Maxim machine gun on its adjustable tripod. The belt of cartridges can be clearly seen. This was the weapon used by the British Army during two world wars and, despite some disadvantages, proved itself in every action.*

Developments in self-loading weapons

THE first country to equip its troops with self-loading weapons was Mexico. The weapon, known as the **Mondragon** after its inventor General Manuel Mondragon, was issued in 1908. It used a mechanical system powered by gas from the explosion and was fitted with a magazine just in front of the trigger guard. The Mexican government lacked the facilities to manufacture the weapon, so they approached a Swiss firm, but before the full order had been completed a revolution overthrew the government and the Swiss were left holding the rifles. They were, no doubt, delighted when Germany offered to purchase them and Mondragons saw limited service during World War I, when they were fitted to some German aircraft. Possibly their most notable use was in 1923 when the patriot, guerilla and bandit Pancho Villa rode into an ambush at Parral in Mexico. The hidden marksmen were armed with Mondragons and Villa and his friends fell dead on the ground before the rain of bullets.

The French also experimented with a gas-operated, self-loading rifle but they dropped the idea and there was little further development until the 1920s.

The Thompson sub-machine gun

MOST machine guns fired a cartridge designed to fit into a rifle, but a number of automatic weapons were developed which fired the smaller cartridge designed for use in a pistol. These light machine guns are usually designated as sub-machine guns; the first was developed by the Italians and was known as the **Villar Perosa**. It fired 9-mm Parabellum cartridges which were those used by the Luger pistol–these were fed in from a curved magazine holding 25 rounds. In the 1920s there appeared what is almost certainly the best known of all sub-machine guns–the **Thompson.** The first production model was issued in 1921 and despite various claims, it seems to have been made only to fire .45-inch cartridges. The magazine came in five sizes: a box magazine holding 18, 20 or 30 rounds and circular drum magazines holding 50 or 100 rounds. "Tommy" guns could be used to fire single shots or, on automatic, for as long as the trigger was depressed at a rate of 800 rounds a minute. A number of slightly varying models were produced to suit different holding methods: the earlier models had pistol grips at the rear and beneath the barrel, whereas later models had a block in place of the forward grip. This sub-machine gun acquired a sinister reputation, for it was popularly supposed to be the weapon of the gangster during the Prohibition era in America. It also saw service during World War II.

The Winchester

ONE weapon which is instantly recognizable by most people is the **Winchester**–often described as "the gun that won the West". The firm was founded by Oliver Winchester, a shirt manufacturer of New Haven, Connecticut, who knew little about guns but a great deal about business. In 1857 he took over the assets of a firm making the Volcanic repeater, a gun using a lever mechanism to load cartridges into the breech. In 1860 his firm made the **Henry rifle,** which had a tubular magazine below the barrel and was reloaded by operating an extended trigger guard. Henry rifles could average one shot every three seconds including time for reloading, and were therefore in demand. In 1866 Oliver carried out a reorganization, renaming the firm the Winchester Repeating Arms Company. Here were produced the first of the Winchester rifles. Cartridges were loaded into the magazine by way of a small gate set in the brass frame near the breech. Mechanically it was a good action and its success was

An Indian scout fires a Spencer carbine using a support. The Spencer was a strong rival of the Winchester.

A Swiss-made, Mexican Mondragon self-loading rifle, fitted with a drum magazine. The action was operated by gas pressure.

Modern version of the Winchester lever action rifle. This one was made in 1967 in honor of the Canadian Centennial and fires a 30.30 cartridge. The loading gate through which the cartridges are fed into the tubular magazine below the octagonal barrel can be clearly seen.

Model 1921 Thompson sub-machine gun with 20 round box magazine of .45-inch cartridges. To cock the action, the top bolt has to be pulled back.

enhanced by the fact that its brass, center fire cartridge also fitted some Colt revolvers. Thus, only one supply of ammunition need be carried for revolver and rifle. A few specially selected weapons were offered at extra cost, marked as 1 in a 100 or 1 in a 1000, up until 1878. Not all Winchester rifles had the famous lever action: the company produced weapons with pump-action reloading as well as single-shot rifles.

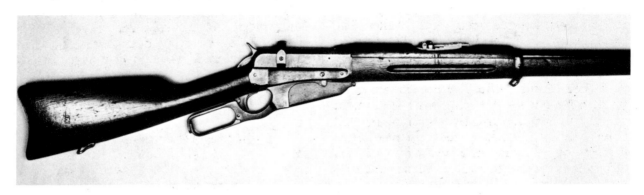

Top *Lever action Winchester Model 95 made in 1915–16 for the Russians and firing a 7.62-mm cartridge. 100,000 were ordered together with 300 million cartridges. This model has a box magazine instead of the more usual under-barrel one.*

Right *Detail of the mechanism of the lever action Winchester rifle; the bolt at the top is operated by the lever and extracts the cartridge as well as cocking the action.*

The Lee-Enfield

THE Snider rifle was the first breech loading rifle issued to the British army, but it was only a stop-gap and in 1871 the **Martini-Henry rifle** was adopted. This had a breech opened by depressing the trigger guard to admit a .45 cartridge. In 1883, a committee was appointed to consider the advisability of adopting a magazine rifle and as a result of their deliberation and tests they recommended a rifle firing a .303 bullet. The barrel was to have rifling as designed by Metford and the action was that of a James Lee of Ilion, New York – the model was known as the Lee-Metford rifle. There was a magazine situated below the breech which held eight rounds pushed upwards by a spring-operated plate. Loading, cocking and ejection were carried out by means of a manually operated bolt which could be moved backwards and forwards by means of a knob fitted on the right.

With the bolt pulled back the magazine was loaded, then the bolt was pushed forward taking with it the top cartridge. This was pushed into the breech and the bolt was then rotated through 90 degrees, thus locking it firmly in place ready for the shot to be fired. The new smokeless powders, with their greater power necessitated deeper rifling and a new barrel developed at the Royal Small Arms Factory, Enfield, outside London, was chosen. This new combination weapon was the **Short Magazine Lee-Enfield** rifle; the SMLE, as it was known, produced in various patterns, was to give excellent service during the two World Wars.

Details of the Lee Metford magazine rifle as shown in the Illustrated London News of February 28th, 1891. Figure 9 is of the dial sight and Figure 8 is of the head of the bolt.

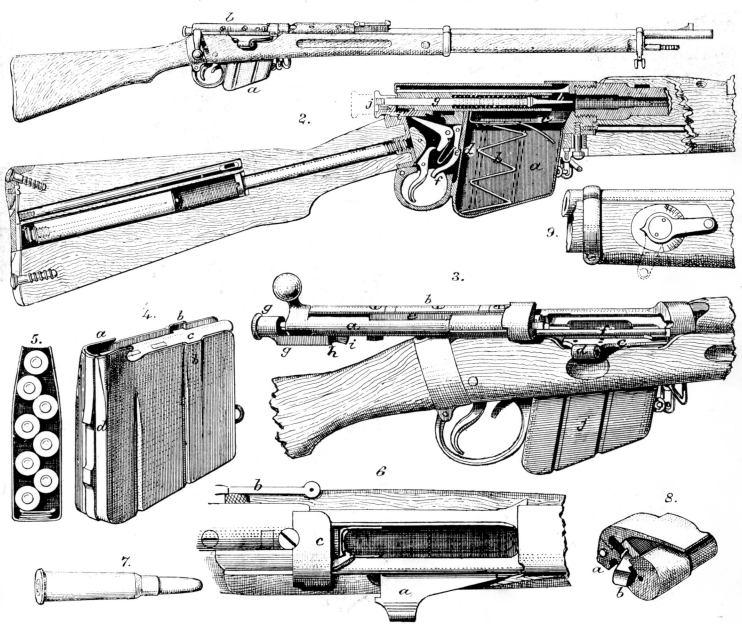

The MP 44, or as it was known later, the STG 44. This was the forerunner of many of the assault rifles in use today.

Machine guns of World War II

DURING World War I, the German forces relied mainly on the Maxim gun which was found to be very serviceable and reliable. When the defeated Germany gathered itself together and began to build up its armed forces once more, it soon started to plan for standard weapons. When war came in 1939, there were still several types of machine and sub-machine guns in use. The **MP (Maschinenpistole) 18,** firing a 9-mm bullet, was in use until 1943 when it was withdrawn from front-line troops. Probably the best known was the **MP40,** issued in late 1940 and made by Schmeisser, which was introduced originally for parachutists but became popular with the entire army. Again, it fired a 9-mm bullet and had a 32-round magazine. It could be fired from the hip, for it had a pistol grip, but there was also a folding skeleton stock which could be opened out for use when firing from the shoulder. The MP40 had no selection for single shots but was totally automatic with a rate of about 500 rounds a minute. In 1943, a new weapon was introduced which was made up of pressed parts, a cheaper quicker means of production than milling. Originally known as the MP43 or MP44, it had a new title conferred on it, that of **Sturmgewehr 44,** as a kind of recognition of its military value. It used a slightly smaller cartridge, 7.92 mm, and had a rate of fire of around 800 rounds a minute.

During World War II the Germans undertook a great deal of research into unusual weapons, particularly into rifles with curved barrels. It was thought that they could be used by tank crews when attacking infantry were on the outside of the vehicle.

German troops used modern versions of many World War I light machine guns, but among the more recently designed weapons was the **Czech 7.92-mm ZB26.** Ironically, this gun came from the same works that supplied the original **Bren gun** used by the British Army. The Bren was an outstanding weapon noted for its reliability and its accuracy, even though it was thought to be rather heavy. It had been modified to fire the standard British .303 cartridge which was fed into the breech from a curved box magazine holding either 30 or, much less commonly, 100 rounds. Each Bren gun had a spare barrel and it was necessary to change the barrel after firing a number of rounds, so hot did it become. The light machine guns, Browning M2 or the 1917A1, were extensively used by American and British forces, particularly in aircraft, where in the heavy bombers they were mounted in batteries of four power-operated turrets.

In the field of sub-machine guns the **Sten** was a most distinctive model, for it was designed to be mass-produced from a minimum of components. It was also unusual in that it was chambered to fire a 9-mm bullet, the first such military arm to be used in Britain.

Below *German STG 44 of World War II. One is the conventional model whilst the other is fitted with a curved barrel and periscope sight.*

Bottom *Cut-away, demonstration model of a .303 Bren gun which clearly shows the cylinder leading the expanding gas down from the barrel and back to the operating mechanism.*

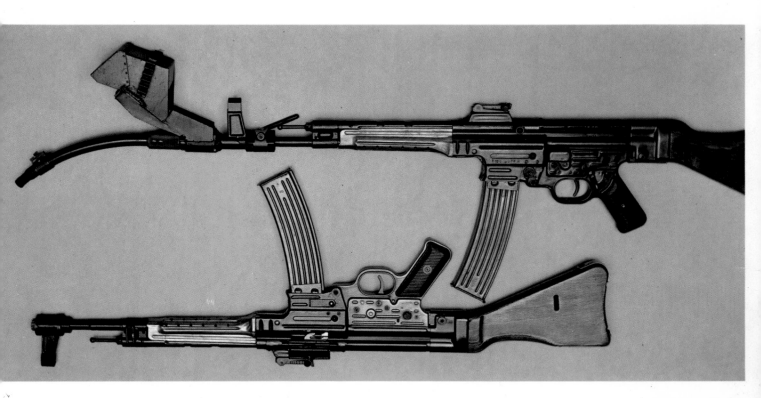

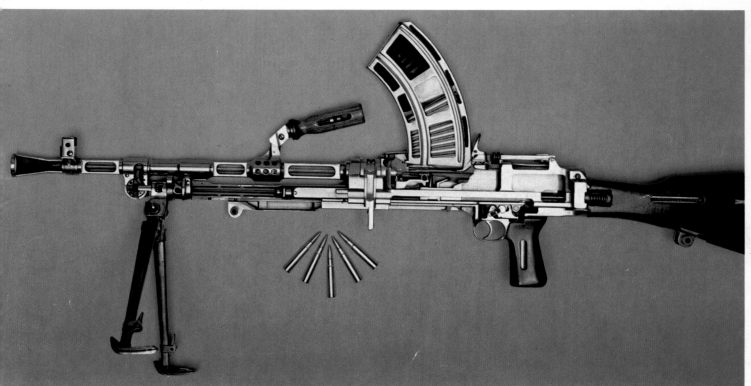

Modern firearms

WITH the adoption of the center fire cartridge, the modern firearm was born and over the last fifty years there have been only minor improvements on the basic design. Modern firearms can be divided roughly into four groups: target, sporting, service and black powder. Sporting guns are undoubtedly the most common and among them may be counted some of the most expensive of modern guns, for top quality pieces are still hand made in the traditional way. There have been improvements in the manner of loading, and repeating shot-guns are not uncommon. **Black powder shooting** is a sport that has grown considerably over the past decade. Basically, the sport is devoted to the firing of genuine antique or modern reproductions of antique firearms. Flintlock and percussion weapons are loaded and fired using black powder and the old techniques. Many of the reproductions are manufactured in Italy and Belgium and are extremely accurate copies.

Service weapons have been under consideration by many countries and there is still some controversy as to which is better, revolver or self-loader. In NATO, the standard sidearm is the **Browning Hi-Power** – a self-loading pistol using a 9-mm cartridge in a magazine which holds 13 shots. There has also been a revival of interest in air weapons, which rely for their power on air compressed by a pump or by some piston action.

SIG 9-mm automatic – one of the finest quality self-loading pistols used today. This particular model, the P210-6, has special target sights fitted and the grips are hand-made (not the standard plastic ones).

Top *Smith and Wesson's .357 magnum revolver. This model is usually known as the Highway Patrolman and is commonly used by many American police forces.*

Center *Some of the cartridges used by this weapon, including two target "wadcutter" ones and in the center the longest one is a magnum cartridge.*

Bottom *A Ruger, .357 magnum Blackhawk, single action revolver. It is modeled on the Colt single action army revolver but differs in several respects.*

Modern handguns

One of the more interesting fields in which there have been changes is that of the so-called **magnum weapon.** This involves the use of cartridges which are far more powerful than the normal ones. The magnum cartridges are made in several sizes but the more common ones are .22, .357 and .44 inches, the last being the most powerful available. Since these cartridges are so powerful, the frame of the revolver has to be stronger in order not to suffer damage and for this reason it tends to be somewhat larger than the revolver frame taking a normal cartridge. The magnum bullet has much greater penetrating power than a normal one and for this reason is favored by many law offices. The size of the bullet has been under constant review, and again, the general trend has been towards smaller rather than bigger diameter bullets. Most modern armies use a bullet around 7–9 mm in diameter for the majority of their weapons.

Sights, too, have been the subject of tests with a great deal of work being devoted to the production of those suitable for night use. These may be of a type with a special infra-red projector and viewer or using the so-called light intensifiers which make use of the available–however minimal–natural light. Telescopic sights for day use have also been developed and are fitted to both rifles and pistols.

AK Assault rifle. Variations on this Russian-designed weapon are used by many Eastern European forces and it has been supplied to a number of underground organizations.

Right Soviet Army instruction in the use of the Avtomat Kalashnikova assault rifle.

Assault rifles

Following World War II there was a great deal of interest in developing a type of automatic weapon which was light, capable of automatic fire and firing a more powerful cartridge than most sub-machine guns. The result was the **assault rifle.** During World War II Germany produced the Sturmgewehr or MP43, which has become the pattern for assault rifles produced in many countries. However, the first assault rifle was designed and used in Russia as long ago as 1907: it used a recoil system and fired a 6.5 mm cartridge. The Russians were impressed by the MP43 and following 1945 they concentrated on producing a similar weapon. The result was the **AK** or **Avtomat Kalashnikova,** named after its inventor, a sergeant in the Tank Corps. The action is operated by gas which moves a piston and can be used for fully automatic or semi-automatic fire. If there is one weakness in this otherwise fine weapon, it is that it lacks a "stay open" action. On most self-loading weapons the action is so designed that when the last shot is fired, the slide stays back in the open position clearly showing that the weapon is empty. The AK lacks this feature: the bolt closes after the last shot so that it is possible to hold an empty weapon without knowing it.

The AK is easily manufactured, sturdy and

An AR 18 Armalite, self-loading rifle firing a .223 inch cartridge from a 20 round magazine, as single shot, semi- or full-automatic. It is very light, weighing only 7 lbs with full magazine.

reliable and has been supplied by the Russians to many countries and movements throughout the world. It fires a 7.62-mm cartridge and can be used as a grenade launcher. A number of models are made with slight variations in, for instance, the butt.

NATO forces also use a 7.62 mm cartridge and **FN rifles** designed by Fabrique Nationale d'Armes de Guerre of Liège, Belgium, still the home of a large firearms industry. This rifle, like the AK, is gas operated and can be used for semi- or full automatic fire. In the United States, development of new weapons is carried out by private enterprise and the latest result is the **Armalite assault rifle.** This

weapon was used extensively by United States forces in Vietnam and elsewhere and has been made for various calibers, including 7.62 mm and .223 inches. The action is gas operated and has an open-bolt position when the magazine is empty. There has been experimentation in the field of machine pistols such as the **Skorpion, Vzor 61, Czech model.** It uses a blowback mechanism and fires a 7.65 mm cartridge in magazines of 10 or 20. It is light, offers automatic or single shot and can either be fired easily in one hand, or the folding stock can be used to give stability. The recoil is very slight and therefore the pistol is less tiring to shoot than many.

.22 Weapons

Apart from service weapons, the most-used weapons today are the rimfire, .22 pistols and rifles. The majority of target shooters use this size ammunition, since it is cheap and freely available. For almost all indoor target shooting .22 cartridges are used. However, the small size does not mean that they are harmless, for they have a considerable power and range. Single-shot rifles are made, but most target weapons have a magazine and a manual bolt action, while versions using pump or lever re-loading actions are available. For the really dedicated and devoted target shooter, rifles are made with specially shaped butts, often fitted with curved ends to fit well around the shoulder. Special hand-holds are fitted and a great variety of sights, including telescopic ones, can be used. The barrels of such weapons are heavy and well made with a variety of riflings. Although they all have the same

diameter, there are a number of different-sized .22 cartridges for rifle and pistol. The smallest is the **.22 BB cap,** which is little more than a percussion cap fitted into a case with a bullet and no propellent, so that its range and power are very limited – but still lethal. At the other end of the scale is the **.22 Winchester Magnum,** but for most shooters the .22 long rifle is the most popular cartridge and is used in pistol and rifle.

Although .22 rifles are generally used, there is a great variety of pistols chambered for a variety of .22 cartridges. The beginner's weapon is the **single-shot pistol,** usually breaking at the breech for loading and fitted with a long barrel. Next comes the usual **match pistols,** which will normally be self-loading weapons with a ten-shot magazine. There is a group known as **free pistols** with butts which are designed to give maximum support and stability to the grip. So complex

and involved are some that the hand has to be inserted, rather like putting on a glove. Barrels are fitted with counter weights which can be adjusted to give optimum balance. Trigger pulls can be set so that only a touch is required to fire a round and so complex have some of these free pistols become that they are no longer really pistols, but rather shooting machines. In addition to the pistols designed for .22 work, kits are available which can be fitted to a full-sized, large-bore pistol to convert it to be used for .22. These kits usually consist of a sleeve, which is fitted inside the barrel to reduce its bore; a new magazine; and usually, a lighter bolt—for the lower powered .22 cartridge could not operate a full-sized one. Revolvers for this size cartridge are made and many shooters display a marked preference for them, claiming that in a self-loader the sliding mass of the bolt can divert the aim slightly.

The smallness and cheapness of construction makes the .22 cartridge popular with target shooters and those who wish to do only casual shooting.

Above *Many non-shooters are familiar with the name of Beretta as the supplier of some of James Bond's weapons. The firm produces a wide range of weapons including these .22 automatic pistols. The main difference between them is in the length of barrel. Although small, the .22 bullet is still lethal and the double-barreled derringer made by Reck is a very powerful, personal defense weapon.*

Opposite top *Arminius HW9 has a swing-out cylinder with an ejector to remove the empty cartridges.*

Bottom *Colt, single action, Frontier Scout with staghorn grips.*

The future

IT is difficult to predict the future course of firearm development, but that there will be change is certain. At the moment, in the military field, the tendency seems to be towards a smaller bullet with its inherent benefit in the reduction of weight so that a larger number can be carried by a soldier. Assault rifles or sub-machine guns have largely replaced the older, single-shot rifles and there may be further developments here. It is possible that the main changes will come in the field of propellents. Rockets of many forms are gradually replacing some forms of artillery and there is already at least one pistol using a miniature rocket. The MBA Gygrojet fires a missile of 12 mm from a six-shot magazine, but to date it still has a number of problems. Unfortunately, the missile takes some little time to build up to maximum velocity and accuracy could well be improved. Similar criticism could equally well have been leveled at the earliest cannon, so it is foolish to surmise. In order to save money, some designers are experimenting with cartridges which have no case, but again there are drawbacks. There will probably be some changes in the materials used in the construction of guns, but it is equally possible that in the future some new form of weapon may be discovered that will make the firearm as obsolete as the bow.

Top *The Gyrojet, which fires a 13-mm rocket "missile" and which may be the prototype of tomorrow's weapon. It is light, simple and efficient but relatively inaccurate.*

Above *The Liberator, .45 pistol, an example of a quickly mass-produced weapon—one million in three months—and of the simplest construction. These single-shot pistols were produced in the USA for resistance groups during World War II.*